DOWN ALONG WITH THAT DEVIL'S BONES

Down Along with That Devil's Bones

A RECKONING
WITH MONUMENTS,
MEMORY, and the
LEGACY OF
WHITE SUPREMACY

Connor Towne O'Neill

ALGONQUIN BOOKS
OF CHAPEL HILL
2020

Published by
Algonquin Books of Chapel Hill
Post Office Box 2225
Chapel Hill, North Carolina 27515-2225

a division of
Workman Publishing
225 Varick Street
New York, New York 10014

Library of Congress Cataloging-in-Publication Data

Names: O'Neill, Connor Towne, [date]– author.
Title: Down along with that devil's bones : a reckoning with monuments,
memory, and the legacy of white supremacy / Connor Towne O'Neill.
Description: First edition. | Chapel Hill, North Carolina :
Algonquin Books of Chapel Hill, 2020.
Summary: "A journalist's memoir-plus-reporting about modern-day conflicts
over Southern monuments to Nathan Bedford Forrest, a Confederate hero
and original leader of the Ku Klux Klan, as well as a personal examination of
the legacy of white supremacy through the US today, tracing the throughline
from Appomattox to Charlottesville"—Provided by publisher.
Identifiers: LCCN 2020016840 | ISBN 9781616209100 (hardcover) |
ISBN 9781643751108 (e-book)
Subjects: LCSH: Forrest, Nathan Bedford, 1821–1877. | Ku Klux Klan
(19th century) | Generals—Confederate States of America—Biography. |
White supremacy movements—Southern States—History. |
Soldiers' monuments—Southern States.
Classification: LCC E467.1.F72 O56 2020 | DDC 322.4/20973—dc23
LC record available at https://lccn.loc.gov/2020016840

10 9 8 7 6 5 4 3 2 1
First Edition

"All wars are fought twice, the first time on the battlefield, the second time in memory."

—VIET THANH NGUYEN, *Nothing Ever Dies*

"They say when trouble comes, close ranks, and so the white people did." —JEAN RHYS, *Wide Sargasso Sea*

CONTENTS

DOWN ALONG WITH THAT DEVIL'S BONES

PROLOGUE

E ver since that bright morning in March 2015, when I came across a Confederate cemetery on a major civil rights anniversary, I've been chasing the story of Nathan Bedford Forrest—the Confederate general's brutal life, his long afterlife, and the fates of four of the monuments that honor him. That chase prompted a personal reckoning, too, and the story, for me, begins and ends with an empty pedestal. The first pedestal was the one I found in Selma's Old Live Oak Cemetery, and the tale starts innocently enough (or so I thought at the time). I was looking for free parking. It was March 7, fifty years to the day since Alabama police officers beat, whipped, and teargassed hundreds of Black demonstrators on Selma's Edmund Pettus Bridge. President Obama was in town to mark the anniversary with a speech and to cross the bridge in remembrance. More than 40,000 other people showed up, too. On my drive into Selma that morning, the streets of the usually sleepy city were suddenly constricted with cars, and the sidewalks were overflowing with people gathering for the event. So I turned into Old Live Oak Cemetery, just two miles from the bridge, figuring I might find an out-of-the-way spot where I could park. Old Live Oak is one of those cemeteries that is so expansive that it has its own system of roads. It's also a bingo board of Old South clichés: shaded by centuries-old live oaks and magnolias bearded by Spanish moss, and with dappled sunlight spilling across the mausoleums. And all around there were signs to alert visitors that Confederate Memorial Circle was closed for maintenance: DO NOT TRESPASS.

I was there to report on the Bloody Sunday anniversary, so I had people to interview, plus I wanted to hear President Obama speak, and I was already running late. But those signs caught my eye. At the center of the Circle, a woman was resealing the brick surrounding a pillar topped by a generic Confederate soldier. Next to her, a German shepherd sat at attention. Workers in jeans and cutoff shirts were putting up a wrought iron fence around an old cannon, and on the far side of the circle stood a tall granite pedestal missing a statue.

These days it wouldn't be the most surprising thing to encounter neo-Confederates at a civil rights anniversary. After Dylann Roof, after Donald Trump, after the man-boys with undercuts Sieg-heiling before his inauguration, after the tiki torches and the Dodge Challenger in Charlottesville, these sorts of juxtapositions have come to feel inevitable, the deep dissonance of the American story floating so much closer to the surface. But on that day back in 2015, I was affronted, yes, but also curious, the way you might feel when passing a bad car wreck. I just wasn't yet aware of the ways in which I was a part of the pileup, too.

I got out of my car and approached.

A woman with hair down to her shoulders, the wisps gone gray, and a man with a long white beard that grazed the third button of his blue coveralls came to meet me, their pace hurried, their eyes wary. The woman, whose name I later learned was Pat Godwin, told me the Circle was closed, that I had to leave.

"Okay if I leave my car here?" I said, then asked if they were standing guard.

It's private property, Godwin said. But her tone was not so much "Get the hell on!" as it was "We can do what we please." So I asked again, and this time she told me they were preparing the grounds.

For what? I asked.

Well, for Forrest, Godwin replied, the answer apparently as obvious as if I had inquired about the color of the sky.

That empty pedestal, she then told me at great length, had once borne a bronze bust of Confederate Army general Nathan Bedford Forrest, but exactly three years earlier, on the weekend of the forty-seventh anniversary of Bloody Sunday, under cover of darkness, the statue had vanished. The theft had sparked a heated yearslong battle over both a replacement statue and the very ownership of Confederate Memorial Circle. Finally, after protests and lawsuits and city council showdowns, the Friends of Forrest (as they called themselves) came away triumphant, with a deed to the land and plans to replace the statue. The time was nigh to unveil their new Forrest monument.

BY THAT WEEKEND in March 2015, I had been living in Alabama for almost two years, but I am originally from Lancaster, Pennsylvania. Think Amish country, whoopie pies, an accent that stretches *oh*s, and a lilt at the end of sentences that makes everything a question. I grew up first on a farm, then on a subdivision that used to be a farm, and was now attending the writing program at the University of Alabama. I had been getting acquainted with my new home against the backdrop of several civil rights anniversaries. I moved into a drafty bungalow that abutted a train switchyard in Tuscaloosa's West End three months after the fiftieth anniversary of George Wallace's "stand in the schoolhouse door"—his infamous attempt to prevent Vivian Malone and James Hood from enrolling at the school where I now apprenticed as a writer. My first week of classes marked the fiftieth anniversary of the 16th Street Baptist Church bombing that killed four little girls in Birmingham. These anniversaries echoed through the present, a moment dominated by stories of voter-suppression efforts and the state-sanctioned murders of Black Americans by police officers. So it seemed only fitting to make sense of my new home by looking to its recent past. In fact, the story that had brought me to Selma that day was a reinvestigation of an unsolved murder from the civil rights era.

The Civil War, on the other hand, seemed distant and remote, while Forrest registered as little more than a joke about the Klan from that old Tom Hanks movie, *Forrest Gump.* He was, in my mind, a dimwitted relic of the defeated Old South. But the Friends of Forrest insinuated a sharper edge to Civil War memory, one that cut closer to the bone. Listening to Godwin's voice harden as she described the pitched battle over this missing Forrest statue made me realize that if I wanted to make sense of this state—hell, to make sense of this country—then I needed to go back another hundred years.

In other words, I needed to study up. That's how the bearded man in the blue coveralls put it, anyway, perhaps noticing the blank look on my face as he and Pat went on about Forrest. His name was Todd Kiscaden and he handed me a homemade brochure. Not to be outdone, Godwin told me that if Todd was giving me readings, then she had some for me, too. From the trunk of her car, she handed me a stack of pamphlets. Some were treatises with titles such as "12 Reasons to Fly the Confederate Flag" and "Forrest Fought for You, Will You Fight for Him?" Others were reprints of propaganda from the era of the civil rights movement. One called the 1965 march to Montgomery an orgy, another claimed that the cold case I was investigating was actually a false-flag operation intended to generate sympathy for the movement. The packet usually went for $13, plus shipping and handling, with proceeds going to the cost of the replacement statue, but Godwin said she was giving it to me for free because we were both writers and she wanted me to have some material to write about. She'd been working on a book, she said: *We Fought with Forrest*. That fight, it seemed, was not just about the Civil War, but about civil rights, a fight still raging today.

Brochures in hand, I headed downtown toward the bridge, brooding on a set of questions about a Confederate general whose face I'd never seen. But his name—three words, two syllables each—had already set its hooks in my head. *Nathan Bedford Forrest.*

THE WALK FROM the cemetery to the bridge was only a few blocks, but it traced a major fault line in the country's ideological terrain, one that was about to send tremors through the country. Down on Broad Street, at the foot of the Edmund Pettus Bridge, people were somberly reflecting on the legacy of racial violence and the sacrifices made to dismantle American apartheid. It was tempting, from that vantage point, to think of the anniversary in terms of progress and optimism. When Barack Obama had visited Selma as a presidential candidate in 2007, he told the crowd that he was there because others had marched, that he counted himself among the Joshua generation—the descendants of the movement's foot soldiers, the Moses generation who had crossed over the Edmund Pettus Bridge. Now he returned to Selma as president, the first Black president. In his speech that day, he listed the places where America's destiny has been decided: Lexington and Concord, Appomattox and Gettysburg, Kitty Hawk and Cape Canaveral. "Selma is such a place," he said. "In one afternoon fifty years ago, so much of our turbulent history—the stain of slavery and anguish of civil war; the yoke of segregation and tyranny of Jim Crow; the death of four little girls in Birmingham; and the dream of a Baptist preacher—all that history met on this bridge."

But President Obama sounded a note of caution, too. Progress, he knew, was not inevitable. His presidency had provoked a fearsome backlash—one that included the so-called Birther movement along with a proliferation of extremist right-wing groups. "We just need to open our eyes, and our ears, and our hearts," he said, "to know that this nation's racial history still casts a long shadow upon us."

Indeed, you didn't need to look far for one source of that shadow. Half a mile from the bridge stood a billboard that invited visitors to tour Selma's "War Between the States Historic Sites." The image on the billboard was of a stern-looking goateed man on horseback: Nathan Bedford Forrest. The caption read "Keep the Skeer on 'Em." The billboard had been papered up by the Friends of Forrest, a group who was, at that moment, just blocks away, spoiling for a fight and preparing to erect a new Confederate monument.

All that history had met once more in Selma.

IN THE WEEKS after the Bloody Sunday anniversary, I began to experience a sort of Baader-Meinhof phenomenon with Nathan Bedford Forrest, seeing him everywhere now that I knew to look. That goateed, scowling face pinned to the corkboard in the gas station where I would often stop for breakfast? Oh, so that's Forrest. The residential street in East Nashville where I parked my car for a weekend of honky-tonking? Forrest Ave. That weird, cordoned-off mound on the University of Alabama's quad that I hustled past late to fiction workshop every Monday? The burnt wreckage of the old campus set ablaze by a Union general before he faced Forrest in Selma. When I called up Madison Smartt Bell, whose time-bending novel *Devil's Dream* paints a vivid, paradoxical portrait of Forrest, he told me that Forrest was like the water you swam in if you grew up in middle Tennessee. I was still new here but suddenly felt sopping wet.

So I started reading all I could about Forrest. In life, I learned, he was a hard-bitten striver. Born into dirt-floor poverty on the Tennessee frontier, he became a wealthy slave trader. Forrest went into business during the "Second Middle Passage"—the era between the outlawing of the transatlantic slave trade in 1808 and the outbreak of the Civil War, when an estimated one million enslaved men and women were sold from the Upper South to the rapidly expanding plantations of the Deep South. "He wanted a way to prosper quickly," Forrest biographer Jack Hurst writes, "and at that time and place there was probably no more profitable field than slave-dealing." So Forrest signed onto America's Faustian founding bargain, making a fortune selling enslaved people down the river from his Memphis slave market. When the war came, he used that fortune to equip a cavalry troop, and fought so viciously in defense of the institution that Union general William Tecumseh Sherman called him "that Devil," while his Confederate colleagues dubbed him the "Wizard of the Saddle." The late Southern historian and novelist Shelby Foote named him one of "two absolute geniuses to emerge from the war." But he also became known as the "Butcher of Fort Pillow" after he oversaw the slaughter of more than one hundred surrendering Black soldiers. By the time he disbanded his troops outside Selma in 1865, he had become the most promoted soldier, North or South, having risen from the rank of private to lieutenant general. After the war, Forrest made occasional efforts at reconciliation, telling his troops they had been good soldiers and they could be good citizens, and late in life, he addressed an African American social club and reportedly experienced a come-to-Jesus moment. But his other postwar activities proved far more consequential and enduring: he was an early adopter of convict leasing and lent his preferred nom de guerre to the newly founded Ku Klux Klan, serving as its first figurehead, the Grand Wizard.

In his symbolic afterlife, Forrest haunts the landscape. In addition to the monument in Selma, there's a statue of him overlooking a cemetery in Rome, Georgia, and a bust surveying the lobby of the Tennessee Capitol. There's the thirty-foot bronze equestrian statue in a Memphis park, under which he and his wife are buried. A county in Mississippi, a city in Arkansas, and a state park in Tennessee all bear his name, along with many streets and schools and buildings. There are thirty-one Forrest monuments in his home state of Tennessee—more than all three of the state's presidents (Andrew Jackson, Andrew Johnson, and

James Polk) combined. Sometimes even a brush with Forrest was enough to get you immortalized, as was the case with Emma Sansom who, as a teenager in 1863, pointed Forrest to a low spot in the Black Creek to cross in pursuit of a Union colonel, outside of Gadsden, Alabama. By way of thanks, the town honored her with a stone statue, her likeness standing with arm outstretched at the foot of the Broad Street Bridge.

While Robert E. Lee might seem the obvious candidate for a Confederate monument—as he was to cities such as Richmond, Charlottesville, and New Orleans—it's Forrest's symbolic importance that is perhaps the better bellwether for how we arrived at our current debates over Civil War monuments and memory. Lee was part of the planter class, a "First Family" of Virginia, the avatar of the Southern Gentleman and a graduate of West Point, while Forrest, born into poverty, was a quick-tempered man of action, disdainful of book learning. Author Andrew Lytle, in reference to his status as the Klan's Grand Wizard, called him the "last ruler of the South." Shelby Foote, perhaps trying to outdo Lytle in his admiration for Forrest, dubbed him "the most man in the world." He's a folk hero, both Everyman and Übermensch. And Forrest's myth is stoked by thoughts of what might have been. Because Forrest enlisted as a private and fought in the often-neglected Western Theater, his skills as a cavalry commander were overlooked for much of the war. But what if Forrest had been given a more prominent role? Could the South have won? A good deal of teeth gnashing and sabre rattling gets channeled into Forrest's mythos. He is the Confederate counterfactual, the great hope of the Monday morning Rebel quarterback who refuses to accept the war's end or outcome. And so through each generation Forrest's legend has only grown. Journalist Tony Horwitz reported in *Confederates in the Attic* that, by the 1990s, Civil War memorabilia retailers were selling five Forrest T-shirts for every one they sold of Lee's.

THE NEWEST ADDITION to the cache of Forrest monuments came just two months after the Bloody Sunday anniversary in 2015. It was another still and cloudless day in Selma when Todd Kiscaden, now dressed in gray wool, pulled a sheet from the pedestal in Confederate Memorial Circle to unveil their replacement bust. A crowd of onlookers, nearly one hundred in all, burst into applause. One imitated the shrill yawp of the rebel yell. From a lectern at the center of the Circle, Pat Godwin announced, "Ladies and Gentlemen, the General is back!"

Three weeks later and some five hundred miles away, on a humid and moonless night in June, twenty-one-year-old Dylann Roof pulled into the parking spot closest to the door of Mother Emanuel AME Church in Charleston, South Carolina, and descended the stairs to the basement, where he prayed with the congregation and then murdered nine parishioners in an attempt to start a race war. After Roof was arrested, images and posts from his blog, "The Last Rhodesian," circulated, detailing his motives and mindset. His blog posts chronicled a sightseeing tour of South Carolina's slave memorials and Confederate monuments. He visited Sullivan's Island, once a major slave port and where Fort Sumter looms in the bay. He visited the Museum and Library of Confederate History in Greenville. He visited plantation slave cabins and the graves of Confederate soldiers. He posted pictures of himself with firearms and with the flags of three apartheid states: South Africa, Rhodesia, and the Confederate States of America. Then he headed for Mother Emanuel.

The Charleston Nine murders, as they came to be known, provoked a national referendum on Confederate symbols. When Bree Newsome Bass, an activist and filmmaker, scaled the flag-pole of the South Carolina State House to remove the Confederate flag, she gave the millions watching a sense of their own ability to join the fight. Soon, protesters from Baltimore to Los Angeles, St. Louis to Tallahassee, were calling for the removal of Confederate monuments as well. There were, according to the Southern Poverty Law Center's count, over 1500 "publicly sponsored sym-bols honoring Confederate leaders" in the country—about seven hundred of which were monuments. They were everywhere, and everywhere they were now under fire.

We mostly think about monuments in terms of their sur-face: who they represent and what they reflect. They are, after all, meant to honor and immortalize the person they depict, often by literally putting them on a pedestal. But the architect Aldo Rossi suggests that a city's monuments also serve as containers for the collective memory of that place. And Roof seemed to under-stand this, drinking from these vessels of American memory—of race and region, of terror and tradition—to steel himself before attempting to spark a race war. In response, activists began to tip these vessels over, their stories spilling down from pedestals and into the streets, schools, city council chambers, and state capi-tol buildings where the meaning and fates of these monuments would be debated.

Forrest's symbolic return to Selma and Roof's terrorism became, for me, inextricable. And so, as activists mounted campaigns to remove Confederate monuments, I began to follow those aimed at Forrest specifically. For the last five years, I've chased Forrest's memory across the country, standing in the shadows of his monuments, talking with the activists fighting to take them down and the admirers working to keep them up, investigating the stories these monuments tell and searching out the ones they withhold—stories of cavalry raids and cemetery standoffs, white supremacist movements and nightmarish sculptures, impassioned campus protests and backroom political intrigue, all amounting to a reckoning of America's past and a desperate struggle for its future.

That journey is chronicled here, in a series of dispatches from the battlefields of our country's symbolic landscape. Four cities, four battles, four monuments, all as fiercely defended as they are protested. Monuments like those dedicated to Forrest were, as Derek Alderman, professor of cultural geography at the University of Tennessee–Knoxville, explained to me, "built for the purposes of communicating who mattered in Southern society and who mattered within American society." In that way, they are a reflection of the times in which they are erected as much as they are a reflection of the times they seek to commemorate. You can think of them, Alderman went on, as monuments to the power of the people who erect them, rather than as solely of the person depicted. They are double-jointed, holding the present in the past, the past in the present. And in all four of these stories, Forrest is deployed into symbolic duty during moments of racial tension. In Memphis, a massive bronze statue of him is erected in 1905, as the city is imposing Jim Crow laws and in the aftermath of Ida B. Wells's investigative reporting on lynchings. In Murfreesboro,

Tennessee, a university building is christened with his name at the height of the civil rights movement. In Nashville, a statue of him goes up in the 1990s as a symbol of the backlash to multiculturalism. And in Selma, a few years later, he is honored just after the city elects its first Black mayor. So, over the last five years, as activists mounted campaigns to remove Confederate monuments, they weren't just taking on specific historical figures, but were taking on long-standing systems of racial, political, and economic power. Following these stories told in marble, bronze, and brick, I've seen the whole of American history blowing through, fanning the embers of a cold Civil War, as they chart an unexpected but revealing account of how we got from Appomattox to Charlottesville—and where we might go next.

WHEN I FIRST started writing about Forrest, I conceived of myself as an outside observer. I would bear witness, document, report on the referendums on Forrest taking place in these four cities. But I came to see a larger proxy war in the offing, one that has engulfed the entire nation and implicated me as well. As I logged thousands of miles in my dusty old sedan, conducted scores of interviews, burrowed into archives, and trudged across battlefields, cemeteries, interstate roadsides, and college campuses to stand before these monuments, I was prompted to ask questions about race that I'd never asked before, had never *thought* to ask before.

So much about American life encourages white people to take our whiteness for granted. It is the stock photo, the room tone, of American life, meant to be conflated with the norm. It's insidious that way. Growing up, whiteness often went without saying. But that's precisely it: it goes without saying because white people don't want to talk about whiteness, don't want to see it, don't want to think about what it means, where it came from, or why we seem to still need it. This assumption gets expressed when people wonder aloud about why we don't have a white history month, or insist that all lives matter. But as I charted the battles over Forrest's monuments, I would come to see how whiteness operated—its prerogatives and its amnesia, its symptoms and its sickness.

There were no Confederate monuments where I grew up in central Pennsylvania. Instead there were a series of charred stone pylons that stretched across the nearby Susquehanna River, just west of my childhood home. In the summer of 1863, in order to prevent Robert E. Lee moving on Harrisburg and Philadelphia, town leaders decided to burn a portion of the Wrightsville Bridge. The whole thing went up in flames. Stymied, Lee regrouped to the southwest. That's why the Battle of Gettysburg happened in, well, Gettysburg. The pylons of that bridge still stand in the water. I used to kayak past them all the time. But even though Lancaster County's riverbank doubled as the Confederacy's high watermark and its southern border was the Mason–Dixon line, I didn't think that history had anything to do with me. I figured I floated above it like a kayak on the river. I felt this way despite how common it was to see Confederate flags affixed to the cabs of pickup trucks or the fact that my ninth-grade-history student teacher began the Civil War unit telling us that it was fought over states' rights. Or even what political strategist James Carville famously said about how everything between Pittsburgh and Philadelphia might as well be Alabama. I never thought about being implicated in any of that history because, well, this was Pennsylvania. Growing up in the North had fostered in me a sense that I was somehow exempt from the legacy of the Civil War and, for that matter, the racial madness of the country.

There were, of course, more pointed moments that should have jarred me from this oblivion. One in particular stands out. Before we moved to Lancaster, my family lived in Philadelphia. As the only white boy in my kindergarten class, I was cast as the arresting officer in the annual Rosa Parks play. And so I pinned on the badge of Officer Day, Montgomery PD, stepped onto the Houston Elementary School stage, and removed Ms. Parks from the bus. (In a similar position the year before, my brother did the same.) By asking me to step into that role, my teacher, Mrs. Goodman, had provided me with an opportunity to see that being white meant something, that it carried a legacy— one forged by violence and injustice but cast as benevolent and benign. For years, though, that lesson was lost on me. I would have to learn the hard way what James Baldwin meant when he wrote that "people who imagine that history flatters them are impaled on their history like a butterfly on a pin and become incapable of seeing or changing themselves, or the world."

The memory of the Rosa Parks play revisited me on the morning that I met the Friends of Forrest. Pat Godwin had grinned when I told her that I was from Lancaster. They were raising money for their new Forrest statue by selling miniatures of the bust, she told me, miniatures that had been cast in York, the city just across the river from Lancaster. A few minutes later, Todd Kiscaden would ask me if I believed in the Tenth Amendment to the Constitution. I nodded, unable to recall what it regarded, but went along with it because it was the Constitution. Suddenly he had me in a tight handshake and congratulated me on being a proud Confederate soldier who believed in states' rights. I recoiled but he only held tighter. *No sir, not me*, I wanted to say. *I'm from Pennsylvania.* But his point was clear. Whether I liked it or not, they were putting this Forrest monument up in my name, too. I was implicated, pinned to Forrest like a sheriff's badge. To tell his story, I would have to revise the story I told about myself.

PART ONE

Forrest Lost and Found

Selma

ONE

A Pronouncement of War

There's a story about Forrest from late in the war that I've come to think of as a parable for his life and for his memory. It is September 10, 1864, just months before the Battle of Selma. The scene, a train depot near the Mississippi–Alabama border. Forrest is deep in thought, planning a raid. It's been almost a year since Lincoln, in his Gettysburg Address, recast the war as the fight to refound the Republic, and just days since Union general Sherman took Atlanta. Forrest's attempts to cut off Sherman's supply lines have proved futile. Soon, Sherman will march to the sea. The Confederate rebellion to perpetuate and expand slavery is a cause increasingly lost. Forrest had enlisted in that rebellion as a private, but by now he's a major general. He'll be promoted once more, before the war's end, to lieutenant general. Unlike many of the other commanders, Union and Confederate, Forrest had never been to West Point, had barely attended school at all. "I never see a pen but what I think of a snake," he has famously said. So while other commanders might see to correspondence, read, or consult with advisors, the cagey, solitary Forrest walks himself into a trance to clarify his thinking.

He tucks his hands behind his back, mutters to himself. His steps inscribe a circle around the squat brick station. A soldier in

Forrest's cavalry spots the pacing general. This soldier has grievances to air, so he approaches and begins his complaint. Without
breaking stride, without winding up, without hardly even looking up, Forrest knocks the soldier unconscious with a single
blow. Another of Forrest's cavalrymen looks on and describes
what happens next in his journal. After the blow, Forrest keeps
walking as if nothing has happened, the soldier writes, "calmly
and unconsciously stepping over the prostrate body each time he
came around again."

Each time he came around again. His monuments have a way
of doing that, too.

I've often thought of this story while reporting in Selma,
and never more frequently than when I was trying to reach the
Reverend James Perkins, Jr. But Rev. Perkins didn't want to talk
about Forrest statues with me. At least not at first. Which is
understandable. You're elected as the first Black mayor in Selma,
the city synonymous with Black voting rights, and less than a
week after your inauguration, a group of Neo-Confederates puts
up a Confederate statue? And not just any Confederate statue but
one of Nathan Bedford Forrest? Then that statue is stolen and,
just after another one goes up in its place, the whole country is
engulfed in a debate about Confederate monuments and some
white journalist with a Pennsylvania number starts calling you?
He was skeptical; my calls went to voicemail. But I figured his
sense of what was at stake in these debates would be crucial. So I
kept calling. I left my card in his mailbox. I spoke with his niece.
And, eventually, Rev. Perkins called me back and heard me out.

I told him that I was using Forrest monuments as a lens to
look at race, memory, and the legacy of the war. And in doing so,

I was coming to some hard truths about my country and myself. He sighed and agreed to meet for an interview.

"That statue," he told me before we got off the phone, "was a pronouncement of war."

Perkins is now the pastor at Ebenezer Missionary Baptist Church. We met for pastries between visits to his parishioners. Perkins, now in his sixties, tall and muscular, was dressed in a maroon and gray raglan shirt and a crisp pair of chinos. For eight years, from 2000 to 2008, Perkins served as the mayor of this small Alabama city. He was inaugurated on the first Monday in October—a day of celebration, of long-held hopes finally realized. And that first weekend in office, he remembered, he was attending a seminar for Alabama mayors in nearby Montgomery when his phone rang. It was a local reporter asking him for comment on the city's new statue.

"Statue?" he remembers asking. "What statue?"

The statue in question was a four-hundred-pound bronze bust of Nathan Bedford Forrest atop a nine-thousand-pound granite pedestal erected in the back garden of a city-owned museum. The morning of the dedication was overcast and threatening rain. A group calling themselves the Friends of Forrest gathered behind the antebellum Vaughan-Smitherman House to unveil the monument. The dedication was a quiet affair, or it was meant to be. Though the statue was going up on city property, the Friends of Forrest had not invited the new mayor to witness the dedication, to listen to the songs, or to hear the expressions of gratitude to the donors who'd helped raise the requisite $23,000. Friends of Forrest spokesman Benny Austin explained to the *Selma Times-Journal* that, "In order to avoid causing any embarrassment or hurt feelings among the citizens of Selma and the Mayor, we decided to keep the ceremony quiet and not to make a big deal out of the affair."

But word had gotten out nonetheless. From the perimeter of the garden, over those speeches, prayers, and songs, local activist Joanne Bland led a group of protesters, singing "We will not go back," to the tune of the civil rights anthem "We Shall Overcome."

Bland had grown up in Selma, had gone to school with James Perkins, Jr., was just eleven when she marched on Bloody Sunday. She had gone on to cofound the National Voting Rights Museum and Institute, a repository of the foot soldiers' history, and now leads tours of Selma's civil rights history. She remembers that she was at home the morning of the dedication when a fax came through. It was from a friend in Montgomery who worked in the media, who was passing along a flyer advertising the new statue.

"As I read it, I became angry," Bland told me. She knew immediately, and all too well, what it meant. "The statue was designed to intimidate us," she said. "I was very upset with it and where it was"—a Confederate monument, on city property, in a predominantly Black neighborhood. It was, as she put it, a slap in the face. So she put the word out. Soon Bland and about a dozen others had staked out the courtyard. A police officer on duty described the ceremony as "a Klan meeting without the hoods," although in fact one protester actually did bring a life-sized puppet decked out in Klansman's robe and hood.

The statue at the center of the garden bore a strong likeness to photographs of the general: his hair wavy and pushed away from his face, revealing a jagged widow's peak and giving him a vague Krusty the Clown aspect. Nonetheless, he was somehow still handsome: the piercing eyes set off by the high forehead, the sharp jaw, and the sunken cheeks. Seeing the statue made it easier to imagine the man who killed thirty men and had twenty-nine horses shot out from under him during the war, who would joke about thus being "one up" on the Union by war's end. Easier to contemplate the suffering in his life and the suffering he created in others; easier to see the way the mouth might have fixed around phrases such as "War means fighting and fighting means killing," and, as he reportedly once asked, "If we ain't fighting to keep slavery, then what the hell are we fighting for?" The sculpture trailed off around the collarbone, leaving his head to float above the six buttons of his double-breasted jacket. The pedestal below named the battles in which Forrest fought, along with a partial list of his nicknames: "Wizard of the Saddle / First With the Most / Untutored Genius / Defender of Selma." This was the part of his history the Neo-Confederates wanted to publicly celebrate: the hard-charging, no-schooling, cunning soldier who, in the last days of the war, sought to defend Selma's way of life. To that list, one might have added "Slave Trader / Butcher of Fort Pillow / Grand Wizard." But his friends in Selma had not. Instead, the pedestal also included the phrase "Deo Vindice"— the Confederate motto that translates from the Latin as "With God as our defender" or "God will vindicate us."

The Friends of Forrest felt that theirs was a righteous cause, Forrest their man, and what's more, they resented the interruptions from the protesters. Joanne Bland told me that one of the attendees even confronted her that day, telling her, "We let y'all have your monument to Martin Luther King."

Let us? Bland says she thought. Let us!? But she paused, composed herself. "I had to leave her in her area," she told me, not wanting to lose control and not knowing where to begin. "Too much is wrong with that."

But the comment laid bare the thinking behind Selma's partition. A city with Black and white neighborhoods, Black and white churches, Black and white schools, Black and white histories, Black and white memories would have Black and white monuments, too.

"Selma's problem," Alston Fitts, who has written two books on the city's history, once observed to me, "is that it has more history than it knows what to do with."

JUST A FEW weeks earlier, James Perkins, Jr., won the 2000 mayoral election in a landslide, receiving 57 percent of the vote. The nine-term incumbent, Joe Smitherman, conceded just a half hour after the polls had closed, prompting a spontaneous, joyful march over the Edmund Pettus Bridge. A three-day celebration of barbecues, parties, and parades led up to Perkins's inauguration on October 2nd. "The man took the shackles off us," one resident told the *Los Angeles Times* after his victory. It was a victory thirty-five years in the making (or, depending on who you ask, more like centuries). But it was also a victory that immediately brought a backlash.

Perkins was born in 1952 and grew up in Selma, his father a schoolteacher, his mother a nurse at the city's Black hospital. In February 1965, after a state trooper shot Jimmie Lee Jackson, a twenty-six-year old deacon taking part in a night march in nearby Marion, Alabama, Etta Perkins was one of his nurses.

The march that came to be known as Bloody Sunday was initially conceived of as a symbolic funeral procession for Jackson, headed for the steps of the state Capitol in a rebuke of Governor George Wallace. On the morning of March 7, 1965, some six hundred people gathered at Selma's Brown Chapel AME, Perkins among them. He was only twelve at the time and remembers that he was under strict orders from his parents to remain at the chapel. So just after two o'clock, he looked on as the marchers departed two-by-two down Sylvan Street. They only made it as far as the Edmund Pettus Bridge.

Because Selma is built on a bluff overlooking the river, the north side of the bridge sits higher than the south, and the roadway inclines toward the center before descending on either side. In other words, you cannot see one side from the other. This meant that the marchers were halfway over the river before they could see what awaited them: scores of police officers strapping on gas masks, mounting horses, and slapping billy clubs against open palms. Less than an hour after the marchers set off, they had returned to Brown Chapel AME where Perkins was waiting, chased by lawmen, seeking refuge both in the church and in the homes of the housing project surrounding it.

The day's violence—the clubs, the tear gas, the state troopers and sheriff's deputies ruthlessly beating nonviolent demonstrators—was beamed into tens of millions of American homes on that night's newscast. The subsequent outrage provided sufficient tailwind for the passage of the Voting Rights Act later that year. The Edmund Pettus Bridge, named for a Confederate general, became an indelible marker of civil rights violence, and of triumph forged out of a symbol of the Confederacy. The city, too, became inextricably linked to the racial violence and subsequent triumph that took place there. As CBS reported soon after the attack, Selma "ceased to be a small Southern town and became a symbol."

Joseph Smitherman, a former appliance salesman, had been elected mayor less than a year before Bloody Sunday, running for office on a pledge to "Get Selma moving again" by attracting new business to bolster their flagging economy. Smitherman had won the 1964 election in a town that was roughly 50 percent Black but that allowed just 2 percent of eligible Black citizens to register. Selma was a microcosm of the broader South—both in the barriers to democracy and the violent lengths to which the white power structure would go to maintain the status quo—and thus the perfect city to stage the movement's push for voting rights. Smitherman, who would later temper his racial views, was at the time an avowed segregationist who, in a press conference after the Southern Christian Leadership Conference arrived in town in January of 1965, referred to the SCLC's leader as "Martin Luther Coon."

The Voting Rights Act, passed that August, prohibited discrimination in voter registration, eliminating literacy tests, poll taxes, and grandfather clauses, and in effect, finally enforcing the Fifteenth Amendment, by then nearly a hundred years old. In Selma, it transformed the electorate. And yet Smitherman remained in power for another three decades. The demographic realities in town forced Smitherman to ameliorate his segregationist stances. He knew he could rely on the white vote and courted portions of the Black community with public works projects and appointments to city government. He ran a shrewd political machine and followed voting blocks and absentee-ballot counts the way some people follow their credit score or body weight.

James Perkins, Jr., graduated from Selma High School in 1971, studied mathematics and computer science at Alabama A&M, then worked as a software consultant in Birmingham. He returned home to Selma to helm veteran civil rights activist F. D. Reese's unsuccessful campaign for mayor in 1984, then left again, this time for an IT job in Washington. "I had been blackballed," Perkins explained, telling me that after the election he received a message from Smitherman bluntly stating that he'd never work in Selma again.

And jobs were becoming harder and harder to come by in Selma. In 1977, the Air Force decommissioned Craig Air Field, resulting in a loss of tens of millions of dollars in annual payroll, along with the money the base spent each year on services from local business, an event from which the city has never fully recovered. And economic decline was followed by more racial unrest. In 1987, the city school district hired Norward Roussell as the city's first Black superintendent. Roussell had grown up in New Orleans, earned a Ph.D. from Wayne State University, and arrived in Selma as a reformer full of ideas to improve the city's schools. But in December 1989, the school board, voting on racial lines, opted not to renew his contract. All five Black members of the board immediately walked out in protest. The board claimed that Roussell was "dictatorial" and "abrasive," but many speculated the real reason was Roussell's attempt to formalize the school's "leveling" process, a previously discretionary system of tracking students into college prep or vocational tracks that placed the large majority of students of color in lower levels, with white students in higher ones. "When he came here, children were being put in classes without regard to their abilities. When he did away with tracking, that was the beginning of the trouble," Sheila Okoye, a school board member, said at the time.

"They want a Black here, but they don't want a Black exercising the authority of the office of the superintendent," Roussell, who died in 2014, told *People* magazine. "All this business about being dictatorial and abrasive—when a Black takes a stand, you're 'dictatorial.' When you are aggressive, you're 'abrasive.' There's a different standard for looking at Black personalities in a leadership role." Outrage ensued. Faya Rose Toure (who then went by Rose Sanders), a prominent and controversial civil rights attorney and activist in Selma, had pushed for leveling to be eliminated completely. After Roussell was fired, she led a boisterous march through the halls of Westview Middle School, interrupting the school day. Then student protesters, Toure's daughter Malika among them, occupied the high school cafeteria, prompting the principal to cancel classes for the duration of the protest. When classes resumed a week later, the governor called in the National Guard. White parents were aggrieved, unnerved by the upheaval. So they fled. By the end of the school year, some 250 white students had withdrawn from Selma High, six hundred from the school system in general. What began three years earlier as a sign of progress ended with the de facto resegregation of Selma's public schools.

Perkins's parents still lived in Selma, and he followed the news in his hometown with interest and dismay. Wanting to be closer to his folks but not yet ready to return completely, Perkins and his family moved back to Birmingham. In early 1992, he left town for a business presentation in Slidell, Louisiana. On the trip he experienced what he can only describe as a "calling." Four days later, as if walking in from the desert, he walked into his kitchen in Birmingham and told his wife they had to move back to Selma— he was going to run for mayor. His wife asked if he had lost his mind. "Except she didn't say it that kindly," he told me.

"It was a very difficult time," Perkins said of the move back to Selma and the ensuing mayoral campaigns. In 1992, Perkins lost the election by 600 votes. In 1996, he lost by just 300. Perkins was discouraged, ready to throw in the towel. It was his supporters, he told me, who encouraged him in 2000 to take one more run at it. By the late 1990s, Selma's unemployment rate was at 12 percent, about three times that of the state average. Then an embezzlement scandal plagued the Smitherman administration when the former police chief, the former city clerk, and Smitherman's nephew all pled guilty to siphoning off $700,000 through fraudulent billings. Smitherman considered stepping down after finishing the term, but at the last minute ("Perhaps by force of habit," as historian Alston Fitts speculated to me) he opted to go for his tenth term. That September, for the third consecutive election, the names Perkins and Smitherman would appear on the ballot.

Mayor of Selma was a coveted seat. Perkins, one of the "Freedom's Children," represented Selma's future and a redemption of its past. He would be the first Black mayor in the city to be in the epicenter of the voting rights movement, and was someone who many hoped, given his background in technology, could jumpstart the economy. Smitherman, meanwhile, didn't just represent the old order, he *was* the old order. Faya Rose Toure captured the public sentiment, at least in Black Selma, with her slogan: "Joe's Gotta Go."

Perhaps sensing his days were numbered, Smitherman ran a desperate campaign, one that a white banker in town described in apocalyptic terms and that further stoked Selma's always-on-edge racial divide. "Selma's their Mecca," Smitherman, who died in 2005, said at the time. "They want Selma because this is where it all happened, where people got the right to vote." But look at other cities that have elected Black leadership, Smitherman told the *Times,* "the towns have gone down . . .You need white inclusion, you need diversity in city government. Let's face it, the whites have the money, the white business people. They tend to pull back when it all goes Black. So that's what I'm trying to get across to the Blacks."

Smitherman's white-knighting fit a pattern in Selma. General Forrest is remembered by the city's white citizens as the Defender of Selma. One hundred years later, Selma's infamous sheriff Jim Clark had pugnaciously defended Selma's (and by proxy the country's) racial hierarchy by denying Black Selmians the vote. Now, Smitherman, who had first come to power under that apartheid system, was vying to keep his seat on the notion that he was saving the city from a Black mayor.

It was to no avail.

On election night, Perkins told a standing-room-only crowd that "this campaign has been about faith and fear, and faith won this campaign." He promised to be a force for rapprochement: "I will not be a mayor for Black Selma," he told the crowd. "I will be a mayor for all Selma. It's time to put the Civil War and civil rights history into a museum."

The new mayor brought a new hope for new possibilities. Could Selma finally get out from under the weight of the past? The answer came just five days later, when the Friends of Forrest erected a statue of one of the Civil War's most infamous figures. Though the monument was conceived of and cast months before the election, and thus not an immediate reaction to its outcome, the statue still spoke to the racial schism that defined the town— evidence that the city's festering racial tension had once more gone septic. Pat Godwin responded to the outcry over the statue by saying they already had permission from the mayor, which turned out to be true. Smitherman corroborated the story, issuing a statement, explaining that "On Friday January 14, 2000, I called Pat Godwin at her office at 4:30 p.m. and told her that I approved the monument project pending the approval of the Smitherman Building Museum Board of Trustees."

Approving the Forrest statue became one of Smitherman's last decisions in office.

FAYA ROSE TOURE's law firm, Chestnut, Sanders and Sanders, is just a half-block down Union Avenue from where the Forrest statue first went up. In 2018, we sat in wicker chairs in the firm's conference room and discussed her reaction to the statue. Toure is now in her seventies, with graying braids and a voice that veers into falsetto when aggravated or impassioned. Her former law partner, J. L. Chestnut, once described Toure as "sensitive, volatile, emotional, and idealistic. She has a tendency to fight every war."

Toure remembered that she was on her way to work that Monday after the dedication when she discovered the statue.

"Just think how a Jew would feel with a statue of a Nazi in their community," she told me. "What the statue said to me was that we were still property. We were still chattel, our lives didn't matter, that our history didn't matter."

So she headed for City Hall to demand that Mayor Perkins remove it. And she wasn't alone in that demand. Perkins told me that constituents from many different groups were telling him to take it down. The business community, he remembers, said, "Get rid of it, Perkins, as fast as you can." One told him to just throw the bust in the river. But others were more moderate, telling him to leave it alone. It was history, wasn't it? And you can't change that. Then, of course, there were the Neo-Confederates, adamantly opposed to any change.

Because it was the city council, and not the mayor, who could determine what could take place on city property, Perkins huddled that Monday night with the nine-member council. Afterward they issued a statement acknowledging Forrest's fraught history and his military acumen, then set forward three options: that the statue be either 1) moved inside the museum without its pedestal; 2) moved to Riverside Park, where reenactments of the Battle of Selma take place; or 3) taken down.

The Friends of Forrest balked at all three options, protesting that they had been given permission by the previous mayor to place the statue where it was. "I remember Mayor Perkins saying that we need to put the Civil War and the civil rights movement in the museum," Pat Godwin added. "That's exactly what we are doing." The controversy dragged on for months. In January, Toure led an offshoot from the Martin Luther King Day march to the statue. She tied a rope to the statue and tried to topple it.

The rope broke before the bronze yielded, but she promised to return every day until the statue was taken down. "If you want to maintain white supremacy a hundred years after the end of slavery, you need monuments and statues and the names of streets to remind people subliminally that [white people] are still in control," Toure told me. "They are trying to perpetuate the past forever."

The statue hung like a 400-pound bronze millstone around Perkins's early days in office. There were major issues to address in town: the unemployment rate, the schools, the dwindling tax base. But he had to do something about that Forrest monument. All three of the initial proposals had proved nonstarters, so Perkins tried another tack: What if they moved the statue to Confederate Memorial Circle? A month later, the council voted 5–4 in favor of the move. Perkins remembered that the swing voter, Jean Martin, received death threats and a brick through her window.

"She was a nervous wreck following that, but it was a courageous vote," Perkins said.

So Forrest took up his new residence amidst the gloomy shade of Old Live Oak Cemetery in the spring of 2001.The Friends of Forrest sued the city, but a federal judge threw out the case in 2003.

DURING THE ELECTION, Smitherman had predicted that if the city elected a Black mayor, Selma's economy would suffer. The morning after Perkins's election, the *Montgomery Advertiser* wrote that Perkins's tenure would be judged by "how successfully he harnesses political and economic power—which aren't held by the same hands in Selma—for the good of the city." But the controversy over the Forrest statue only heightened the divide. He had pledged to be a uniting force, a feat that was already a challenge in Selma and became nearly impossible with such a bitter, public debate over a figure like Forrest.

During Perkins' first term, the white flight only accelerated. In 2000, the town's population was about 65 percent Black. Today it is approximately 80 percent. After the school protests in 1990, many white families moved, headed for the county school system. More joined them after the election. Residents of Valley Grande became anxious that Perkins might annex them into the city as a revenue source, so they incorporated as a town in 2003.

Coming at a moment of rapid resegregation, the message sent by the Forrest statue was clear to Joanne Bland: "That racists are still here. That [they] still have the same power." Every time she sees the statue, she swears she sees the lips move: "You're so mad but I'm still here."

"Ain't that a blip?" Bland asked me. To her, the white flight, and resultant hit to the city's tax base, was like the economic equivalent of erecting a Forrest statue in a Black neighborhood. "It's like they're trying to let us die," she lamented. "That's what I'm trying to understand: why are you trying to kill Selma?"

At the very least, Bland said, "If you don't want to spend money here, live here, then take [Forrest] with you."

"Selma is a battleground," Perkins told me. "April of 1865, the last significant battle of the Civil War, was fought on that ground. That makes Selma iconic. . . . So the battle to regain Selma never stopped. This was a continuation of a battle that started way back in the 1800s. And they had the same general."

TWO

The First Battle of Selma

After Rev. Perkins told me that the dispute over the Forrest monument in 2000 was a continuation of the same battle from 1865, I felt compelled to see that first battlefield for myself. It was, according to Google Maps, just west of downtown, a half-mile past the cemetery on Dallas Avenue. What I found, though, was your basic city park: a baseball field, a walking trail, some concrete grills. Totally unassuming stuff. Nothing there to suggest a battlefield, much less the hallowed ground of the "Wizard of the Saddle." I had to interrupt several morning joggers, inquiring about the location of the battlefield, before I knew to meander down a narrow, cracked concrete path off the main road that runs through the park, past the pavilions, to its end, at the foot of a rotting red covered bridge. I crossed over and emerged onto a nondescript meadow, long and sloping, which extended down from the ranchettes high above on Riverside St. to the muddy beach where the creek meets the Alabama River.

Where the hillside evens out onto the meadow, there's a line of fortifications, a zigzag of timber that runs along the field. It was brambled through with privet, wisteria, and switchgrass and looked like the ragged net of a long-neglected tennis court. Fortifications like these, miles of them, had surrounded the city during the war. The city was so well fortified because there was so much to protect. Before the war, Selma—known as the Queen City of the Black Belt—was a financial center in that fertile strip of soil that cinches the middle sections of Mississippi, Alabama, and Georgia. The city was officially incorporated in 1820, and that year's census reports 3,324 white people in Dallas County, who had brought with them 2,679 enslaved Africans. After that, the city took off. Cotton plantations sprang up across the Black Belt. Selma became a major railroad crossing and, on the banks of the Alabama River, a well-situated port for river trade. Plantations sent daily shipments of cotton down the river to Mobile and on to textile mills in Boston and Providence. By 1860, there were 7,780 white people and 25,840 enslaved people living in Dallas County.

When you tally America's assets in 1860—the railroads, the manufacturing, the steel and iron, the cotton—all of them combined were worth less than the market value of those held in slavery. In *The Half Has Never Been Told*, historian Edward E. Baptist lays out how "slavery's expansion shaped every crucial aspect of the economy and politics of the new nation." Baptist notes how settlers headed into the newly opened Deep South with "Alabama fever": the sense that "every white person who could get frontier land and put enslaved people to work making cotton would inevitably become rich." Nowhere was this more true than in the Black Belt. Dallas County was the leading cotton producer in the state. In forty years, a single generation, Selma helped reshape the country: its economy, its landholdings, its textile mills, its moral debts. And by 1860, Selma not only generated the wealth extracted from the labor of those enslaved in the Black Belt fields, but also produced a great many of the weapons used to defend their right to do so. It was home to one of the largest war machines south of Richmond's Tredegar Iron Works; its factories produced munitions and its foundry made ironclad ships for the war effort.

And when the war came, Selma's Magnolia Cadets marched out of town carrying a Confederate flag made by Elodie Todd Dawson. Yes: Todd—the half-sister of the Todd you might be thinking of. The Todds were Lexington, Kentucky, elites, a landed, wealthy, slaveholding house divided. Mary Todd had married that pensive, ambitious lawyer, Abraham Lincoln, up in Illinois; her half-sister Elodie married the handsome, fire-eating lawyer Nathaniel H.R. Dawson, down in Alabama. Nathaniel—passionate, sharp-tongued, sensitive—was a major advocate in the Alabama Secession Convention. Elodie—dark hair in ringlet curls, secessionist to the hilt—sewed the flag for Dawson's infantry unit. They had met at the inaugural ball for Jefferson Davis, affianced in secret, and corresponded almost daily through the war.

Lieutenant General Nathan Bedford Forrest arrived in Selma at dawn on April 2, 1865, covered in blood from head to horse's hoof. He was in retreat from a running battle through Cahaba the day before. Forrest had dispersed many of his troops to refit after the losses of the Middle Tennessee campaign in late 1864, and so it was with depleted ranks that the general, once thought invincible by the Union Army, attempted to defend Selma.

NATHAN BEDFORD FORREST's early life in many ways mirrored the growth of the frontier where he was raised. Born in Chapel Hill, Tennessee, on July 13, 1821, the same year as the last treaty in Andrew Jackson's Indian Wars, he was the eldest of

William and Mariam Forrest's brood. Fanny, his twin, like two of his brothers and two more of his sisters, succumbed to typhoid. But Nathan lived. By age thirteen, three years after President Jackson's Indian Removal Act sent the Creeks, Chickasaws, Seminoles, and Cherokees west on the Trail of Tears, the family moved to a modest hill farm in northern Mississippi. By sixteen, after the death of his father, Nathan became the man of the house. There's a story of an all-night cougar hunt to avenge his mother after she had been attacked by the cat while coming home with a basket of chickens. Forrest's hounds trailed the cougar and treed it, then he waited for hours until daybreak to draw a bead before returning home to present the fresh-skinned pelt to his mother. When his younger siblings came of age and his mother was set to remarry, Forrest went full-time into trading. He worked at a modest livery stable and farm-supply store, and was a small-time trader in livestock and enslaved people. He had only a few months of school to his name, but his business instincts were strong, his arithmetic stronger, his ambition strongest.

Seeing his success, his uncle Jonathan took him on as a partner in his livestock trading business. Young Nathan was on the rise. But on a street corner in recently incorporated Hernando, Mississippi, in March 1845, it all changed for Forrest. Three Matlocks, brothers and planters, confronted Jonathan Forrest. He owed them money. An argument broke out. Things escalated quickly. Shouting. Shoving. Then one of the Matlocks drew a gun. Nathan stepped between them and was faster on the draw, putting a bullet in one Matlock's shoulder, another in the arm of his brother. But his pistol held just the two bullets. Momentarily stymied, he caught a bullet in his right arm. A bystander threw him a knife, and he rushed the third Matlock. They grappled to a stalemate. But then Jonathan Forrest cried out—one of the Matlocks' bullets had found his chest.

The wound proved fatal. Jonathan Forrest's business was now Nathan's. Except the business was failing. That day, just before the deadly confrontation with the Matlocks, Jonathan had mortgaged all he owned: five enslaved people, a stock of horses, cattle and sheep, a wagon and seventy-five barrels of corn. Jonathan Forrest owned no land but owed money all over town: "greater as I apprehend than I will be able to pay" to "divers other persons." When Jonathan died on the streets of Hernando that afternoon, Nathan Bedford Forrest became the sole owner of the business and thus the holder of this debt. That the two events—the mortgage and the duel—are connected is difficult to prove, still more difficult to ignore.

But Forrest was a striver. And he'd come this far. He wanted a life better than the one into which he'd been born. The Deep South in those years was one like big boomtown. Fortunes were made and plantations carved out of the pine woods daily. Settlers came over the mountain in droves, with coffles of enslaved people clinking shackles just behind. Land grants were cheap, cotton prices were high. At that moment, in that setting, the unschooled, unrefined young man saw an inside track to wealth and prosperity. It must have seemed so close he could hardly fail to grasp it.

So the striver did what strivers do: he kept moving forward, debt be damned. A month later he bought a house—a modest but well-appointed home in downtown Hernando. Two months later, Jack Hurst writes in his biography of Forrest, he was riding up to a creek ford outside town when he saw a carriage run off the road and into some mud. Inside was Mary Ann Montgomery and her mother. Forrest knew of Mary Ann but had no standing—social or economic—to call on her. He sensed his chance. He dismounted and put his shoulder to the carriage wheel alongside the Montgomerys' driver. Together they heaved it from the muck. Such a gallant display—especially when performed while two dandies and would-be suitors watched on horseback, afraid to ruin their calfskin boots—provided Forrest his opportunity. He asked then and there, while muddied to his waist, for permission to call on Mary Ann. He came around the next week, chased the same two young men from the Montgomerys' porch, and proposed. Mary Ann demurred at first, but Forrest showed up to their third meeting with marriage license in hand. Mary Ann's uncle and guardian, the Reverend Cowan, was skeptical, too. "Why, Bedford, I couldn't consent," he told Forrest. "You cuss and gamble, and Mary Ann is a Christian girl." I know, Forrest replied, "and that's just why I want her." He proved persuasive. The two were married that May, accompanied, as the Hernando newspaper wrote, "by a good sweet morsel of cake and a bottle of the best wine."

In 1852, the Forrests headed for Memphis, the inland capital of the slave trade. "I will pay more than any other person," Forrest advertised, "for No. 1 NEGROES suited to the New Orleans market." In Memphis, Forrest made his fortune, with one thousand enslaved people passing through his "negro mart" every year. Using that fortune, he equipped his own cavalry troop when the war came, and in 1862 advertised that "those who know Forrest, who are acquainted with his reckless bravery controlled by a fund of sound and logical sense" should join up. Forrest wanted soldiers seeking the opportunity to "have some fun and kill some

Yankees." Through his military maneuvers, he distinguished himself as a shrewd cavalry tactician: cunning timing at Fort Donelson, a daring rearguard action at the Battle of Shiloh, an outnumbered upset at Brice's Cross Roads. The uneducated rube from Memphis became the highest-promoted soldier in the war.

But by April of 1865, the Battle of Selma was a last-ditch effort. It would have taken 20,000 to adequately man the ramparts in Selma. Forrest had only 4,000, mostly old men and young boys. Union general James Wilson had with him 13,000 troops, among them the defector who had designed Selma's fortifications, and he also had an intercepted letter describing where and in what number Forrest's troops were stationed. He had first sent a regiment to Tuscaloosa with instructions to torch the University of Alabama, known as the West Point of the Confederacy, then turned his heels on the smoldering campus and headed south for Selma, then one of the last standing Confederate arsenals. Wilson's troops arrived at 4 p.m. Within half an hour, the Union flag flew above the city's outer defenses. Two subsequent charges at the inner walls led to an hour of bloody hand-to-hand combat. By dusk, the city had fallen.

Federal forces proceeded to raze Selma. "I assumed the command of the city on Monday . . . and commenced destroying everything which could be of benefit to the enemy," wrote Brigadier General Edward Winslow. Union troops burned Selma's arsenal, the foundry, the ironworks, the horseshoe and shovel factories. They emptied whiskey barrels into the street. Then they headed east. Selma fallen, the Confederacy soon followed. Union troops took Richmond the same day. A week later, Lee was in the judge's chamber of the Appomattox courthouse;

then Wilson captured Jefferson Davis in eastern Georgia. The war was over.

    I WANDERED DOWN to the bank of the river and tossed a few stones. It wasn't much of a battlefield and it hadn't been much of a battle. "Defender of Selma"? The Yankees took the town in just a few hours, dumped the whiskey, destroyed everything of benefit to the enemy. But this is what Rev. Perkins was saying. Forrest lost the battle, but the war about what that loss should mean was still raging. I was coming to see that Civil War history was a stand-in for something more emotional, a way to channel anxieties about entitlement, possession, control. Down by the banks of the river, I found a pile of timbers similar to the ones used in the fortifications, as if the city stood ready to close ranks at a moment's notice.

    Having seen the actual battlefield, I crossed back over the covered bridge and got in my car. But when I reached the main road, I wasn't ready to leave. So instead of turning right toward the exit, I headed left, deeper into the park. Back beyond a water treatment plant, I found a restaurant overlooking the river. It was raised up on flood-proof stilts, and the ramp up to the second-story dining room switched back and forth at least six times, with hardly any incline—it was like walking up a hamster wheel. I ordered a Bud Light and apologized to the bartender for tracking some mud into the room. I had been out at the battlefield, I explained. She nodded and told me that most of the fighting had actually taken place on the other side of Dallas Avenue, where the country club is now. (A country club that is still all white; not that she mentioned that.) A couple down the bar overheard our conversation and chimed in. They told me that they used to sit out on the porch of a friend's house that overlooked the battle-field. Great parties during the annual reenactments, they said, a little wistfully. The city owns the park and has started to charge fees, thousands of dollars, to hold the reenactment. It just hasn't been feasible in recent years, they said with a sigh. I went back to nursing my beer.

THIS HAD BEEN my first trip to a battlefield other than Gettysburg, which is a National Military Park. To go there is to *go* there. There are park rangers, a visitor's center, a massive 360-degree "cyclorama" painting of Pickett's Charge. It's ground hallowed by Lincoln himself. Which entails a cordoning off. Physically, obviously, but also psychically. The battlefield is not enmeshed into the fabric of daily life of Central Pennsylvania as it is in Selma, where people were, at that moment, playing rounds of golf on land where the battle was fought, or drinking whis-key gingers and complaining about the fees to reenact a battle to which they once had porch-side seats. It gets dropped so often as a cliché about the South, how the past is never past, but that's true everywhere. What seemed more distinctive was how the past intruded into daily life here in such persistent, immediate ways.

At the time I was supporting myself by working as a land-scaper. It was a small outfit, just three guys, and we did mostly home-sprinkler maintenance in the Tuscaloosa suburbs. When work was slow, our boss would find "honey-do's"— small per-sonal jobs—to help us hourly workers make enough for rent. He was kind like that. But every once in a while, on these jobs, the state's fraught history would spill out like a busted pressure line.

Take one day, just a few months earlier, over in Demopolis, a few towns west of Selma. We were clearing brush and doing some upkeep on an old mausoleum. It was in the family plot of our boss's mother's side—"Family business," as our boss put it, shrugging, as if he were asking us to shovel out a few yards of mulch in his backyard. Allen Glover, the man for whom the mausoleum was built, wasn't just an ancestor, he had actually founded Demopolis in 1819, when he and his brother and the seventeen people they had enslaved came to the canebrakes of Alabama from the South Carolina low country. By the time the war came, the enslaved people on the Glover family's 3,000-acre plantation were bundling enough cotton for the Glovers to afford their own steamboat. It was one thing to read about this history, quite another to prune the crepe myrtle that shaded the grave of the man who made that happen in Marengo County. Whether in the parks where you played baseball, or at the jobs you worked for rent money, the past was inescapable and always underfoot.

Granted, to approach this history with the binary framework provided by the Civil War can make for a simplistic morality play. One in which it's all too easy and too obvious for a Yankee to traipse into a Southern cemetery and clutch his Northern pearls. Robert Penn Warren called this instinct the "treasury of virtue"— the white Northerner's feeling that, by dint of our affiliation with the Union, the great, emancipating army, well, then we were (and remained) morally upstanding, unimpeachably good. It was a feeling that could render us "happy in forgetfulness," the Civil War like an event horizon beyond which our own pasts vanish.

But what were we forgetting? What was reflected in the markers of my own family's history that we'd rather not look at? I grew up in Central Pennsylvania, but it was my mother's New England ancestry that loomed. And with good reason: Plymouth Rock, the gallows at Salem—these were the monuments to which we traced our roots. My mother's line claims two passengers on the Mayflower, and we are directly descended from Rebecca Nurse (née Towne), whom you might know as Goody Nurse, the elderly midwife hanged as a witch in Arthur Miller's *The Crucible.* Her sister, Mary Esteys, also stood trial and was sent to the gallows that year. "The Witchcraft Delusion," my great-grandfather George writes in the genealogy he compiled, "took a heavy toll of this family." A reference guide at the front of that genealogy also lists "Soldiers in the Indian and Colonial Wars," "Soldiers in the Revolution" (with special emphasis on those that "Respond[ed] to Lexington Alarm"), along with those "Massacred by Indians" and those who were "Scalped but Recovered."

I have a copy of the genealogy, which was completed and published by my grandfather. It's a lovely, leather-bound book, the title *Ancestry Of My Parents* embossed in gold on the deep maroon cover. I took it down from the shelf recently and a folded piece of paper fell into my lap, a note in my mother's handwriting. On one side she'd drawn a family tree and on the other set down some reflections—"Legacy," she titled it. In it, she describes her father as "a man whose past engulfed and consumed him." He was a man, my mother writes, "born to the wrong century." In his view, the past was a better time and he looked upon it with admiration and longing.

I never met Grandpa Towne; he died before I was born. Even so, growing up I absorbed his misty-eyed reverence as if by osmosis. His was the prevailing attitude reinforced annually on Patriots

Day, Independence Day, Columbus Day, Thanksgiving. Pilgrims, puritans—these were my people. Pious, sacrificing, persecuted people, blown across the Atlantic on the winds of the Enlightenment, fleeing from and then rebelling against tyrants to establish a new nation founded on liberty. They were people who disembarked the Mayflower onto Plymouth Rock, who refused to renounce their God even as the hangman approached. People whose valor made the colonies possible and whose ideals of freedom and democracy were the bedrock on which this nation was built.

That's how the story goes, at least in the "don't think about it too much and pass the cranberry sauce" version. Conveniently, it leaves out the fact that the first enslaved African brought to New England was brought to Salem. Or that nearly half the wealth of colonial New England was generated by enslaved people on the sugar plantations of the West Indies. Or that my ancestors who lost their scalps did so while embarked on a campaign of displacement, dispossession, and destruction of the native peoples from whom they'd stolen the land that became their city on the hill.

We don't talk about that part so much. Still, you can catch glimpses of the other half of this story while paging through the Towne genealogy. The book is peppered with references to "freemen." Rebecca Nurse's life, as recounted before the magistrates in 1692, is described in terms of "purity and goodness," while her sister Mary "recall[ed] the perfect spirit of the Prisoner at Calvary." And Mary's accuser, Mercy Short, claimed to be tormented by the Devil, whom she described as "a Short and a Black Man . . . not of Negro, but of a Tawney, or an Indian colour." Free, pure, Christlike; tawny, black, the Devil—these were their notions of *self* and *others*. And it is by this formula that the early white Americans could abide the contradictions inherent in founding a nation based on principles of life and liberty on property that was stolen land. And by this formula they could justify the enslavement of others on that land.

This is the most enlightening and discomfiting part of reading Edward E. Baptist's book about slavery and the growth of American capitalism: how implicated the North is in the story. To be sure, far fewer enslaved people were brought to the Northern colonies, and yes, slavery was abolished in the North earlier than in the South. But still, Northern businessmen availed themselves of the profits of the slave system at every level and, in so doing, transformed the country into an industrial behemoth. Bankers, creditors, investors, speculators, and industrialists all had a vested interest in slavery's perpetuation and expansion. Pointing out that most Northern Unionists opposed emancipation in the run-up to the Civil War, Baptist posits that white American power struggles in that era were "on one level not driven by a contest over ideals but [by] the best way to keep the stream of cotton and financial revenues flowing." That wealth flowed from the fields surrounding Selma into the bank vaults of New York, and the cotton traveled to the mills of Providence and Boston and, further inland, to Framingham (where my grandfather later worked while he completed the Towne genealogy). Northerners were distanced from the violence, from the inhumanity of the practice, but were implicated all the same. I'd been trudging through Alabama's cemeteries, battlefields, and archives, but the history I was encountering wasn't someone else's, it was mine, too. The more I came to know Selma, the more I was coming to know the country, my family, myself.

To help me to understand what it was like to live in Selma, historian Alston Fitts asked me to imagine what it would be like to be reminded, every year on your birthday, of the worst thing you'd ever done. Up north, we'd rather pass the cranberry sauce, happy in forgetfulness. The distance afforded by the financial instruments of nineteenth-century capitalism persists to this day in Northern memory. It took my moving to Alabama and reporting this book to realize a hard truth about home, a place that suddenly felt both farther away and closer at hand.

THREE

Monument Is Now Headless

March 12, 2012, was a typical day at work for Michael Pettaway, superintendent at Selma's Old Live Oak Cemetery. He met his work crew that morning, and they set about tending one of the many paths that meander the grounds—regular Monday stuff, odd jobs maintaining the plots where the mausoleums loom and the Spanish moss hangs low. All typical, that is, until someone on his work crew asked, "Where'd the head go?"

Pettaway looked up, at a loss for what his employee was talking about until he, too, realized that the Forrest bust had vanished from the pedestal. No one could remember seeing it since the previous Friday. When I reached Pettaway a few years later, he explained to me that, back then, he was cautioned to avoid blowing gravel onto the pedestal, but he didn't exactly make a habit out of looking at the statue every day. At some point over the weekend, though—the weekend that marked the for-ty-seventh anniversary of Bloody Sunday—someone had come to Confederate Memorial Circle and stolen the Nathan Bedford Forrest statue from its eleven-year home.

MONUMENT IS NOW HEADLESS read the headline in the next day's paper.

Confederate Memorial Circle was now a crime scene. The image accompanying the newspaper article depicted an officer dusting the empty pedestal for prints. On closer inspection, eight holes remained where once securing bolts held the 400-pound bust in place, suggesting to Selma Police detectives that it was removed without the aid of a sledgehammer. Wherever the bust was, it was intact.

The Friends of Forrest first offered a $20,000 reward for information leading to the statue's return. When this bounty on Forrest's head produced no leads, they upped it to $40,000. By the time I started looking into this story, it had been years since the theft, but even so, Pat Godwin was still fulminating about it. I reached her at home on the plot of land south of Selma she calls Fort Dixie, where she holds an annual celebration of Forrest's birthday and where the answering machine informs callers that she and her husband can't come to the phone because the genocide against Southern culture is still ongoing and they're out there fighting. At the mention of the statue's theft, Pat Godwin went on a tear, as if the statue had gone missing just a few days ago rather than several years. Godwin had always suspected Toure of being behind it. Toure denied the accusation, offering, in turn, to represent the thief for free.

"I didn't have anything to do with it," Toure told me. "I wish I could have done it. I don't have the strength." I asked if she had a theory about who did. She replied that, for a while, she wondered if the Friends of Forrest had stolen it themselves—to raise money and attention—but eventually came to think that "some righteous Black people said this is sick and we're not going to allow this statue to be on public property in the Black community. I truly believe that."

An anonymous informant tipped off Selma police that local activist Sherrette Spicer had footage of the theft on her cell phone.

Like Toure, Spicer hosted a radio show in Selma. She also led tours of visiting school children, taking them to civil rights landmarks such as the courthouse, the bridge, and the battlefield, and to the statue as well, "to give a cohesive view of everything," she explained. In the months after it had vanished, the bust became a frequent topic of conversation on her radio show. She'd complain on air, tongue in cheek, about how she missed not being able to sit on him or take pictures of him during tours. But then rumors began to circulate that she was using the bust as an ashtray in her apartment above the Slavery Museum downtown. Officers came to her day job, at a call center in Montgomery, with a warrant and left with her phone.

IN THE MEANTIME, the Friends of Forrest set about replacing the statue and, while they were at it, renovating the Circle. The plan that summer was to raise the Forrest pedestal to eleven feet, erect a wrought iron fence around it, and install lighting and twenty-four-hour camera surveillance. That summer, Todd Kiscaden, who lives in Tennessee, and his crew worked on the renovations on the Circle. In mid-August, they marooned the Circle's central pillar to dig out a frame in which to pour a concrete ramp.

Or that was the plan, anyway, until Toure, her husband the longtime state senator Hank Sanders, their daughter Malika Sanders-Fortier, Sherrette Spicer, and some twenty other protesters marched into the cemetery. Though the statue's move to the cemetery had been preferable to its original post at the Smitherman house, it still rankled. Selma, Spicer explained, is a city where lots of people walk to where they need to go and, because the cemetery bisects two neighborhoods, it gets a lot of foot traffic. "It's one thing to walk through the cemetery, it's another thing to have a statue of a Klan leader in it."

"Here are these white people bold enough to come into a majority-Black community—on one side [of the cemetery] is public housing and, on another side, a middle-class community," Toure said. That summer presented a tipping point: there was at present no monument to Forrest but a plan afoot to build an even bigger statue, and she realized she now had a only a small window of time in which to act. No way would Forrest come around again, not on her watch. "I was prepared to go to jail or do anything to stop it."

Anything, that day in August, meant lying in the freshly dug trench that was about to be filled with concrete. Others threw shovels, turned over paving stones, and kicked dirt. The police arrived and shut down construction for the day while the protesters circled the central pillar, holding signs reading "I'm mad as hell and I ain't going back," and "KKK Mindset of Nathan B Forrest Killed Trayvon." Toure vowed never to let the statue return. Kiscaden, furious, complained of losing nearly $600 in cement, while Godwin insisted that the protests were a distraction from the investigation into the missing statue.

Toure soon returned to Confederate Memorial Circle, this time to take pictures of the work site, hoping that her presence might provoke a reaction from the workers that might get them arrested. So Toure marched into the construction site as a crane was operating, tromping into the "hard hat area" without a hard hat. Kiscaden confronted her. Toure claimed that he shoved her, Kiscaden that he was trying to move her away from the dangerous equipment. The spat led the chief of police to again shut down construction and Toure to press charges against Kiscaden.

Amid complaints from both prosecution and defense over who would hear the case, local judge Vaughan Russell stepped in.

"Both sides agreed that I would be acceptable," Russell told me, as Pat Godwin was "someone that I get along with personally but not politically. I get along with Rose politically, but not personally."

The case hinged on video footage Toure took before and during the altercation. While there was some evidence of Kiscaden confronting Toure, "There's a duty on the part of the people to provide safety," Russell said. More tellingly, however, (or, as Russell put it, "One of the most determinative pieces of evidence") was the audio at the start of the video, in which Toure announced her intentions to provoke the construction workers and to have them jailed. So Russell found Kiscaden not guilty.

When I reached Russell at his law practice in downtown Selma, he was quick to register his exasperation with the strife over symbols in Selma.

Selma is one of the poorest cities in one of the poorest counties in one of the poorest states in the nation, he explained. "People come here from Washington to kiss the Blarney Stone, so to speak, but they don't employ people . . . People will come and march but they won't open a factory." He feels like Selma has been scapegoated. Since the 1960s, the city's name has become synonymous with racial violence and voter suppression, as if such attributes were unique only to Selma. And it's this reputation, Russell says, that continues to contribute to the city's economic malaise. Who would want to build a factory in a town with a past like that?, the logic goes. To Russell, these systemic issues make the debate over a statue in a cemetery seem frivolous.

But to others, like Toure, the two are inextricably joined—the broader inequities make the statues all the more egregious.

"People don't get the connection between the symbolism in that statute and the spirit that it represents," Toure insisted. "The people who support those statues, those are the people on juries, those are the people in government, those are people who are police officers, those are the people who are sheriffs. It impacts who gets justice and who does not."

And in a criminal justice system already racially skewed, such a symbol adds insult to an already grievous injury. The incarceration rate in Alabama has tripled since 1978 and more than half of those incarcerated in the state are African American. It is statistics such as these that led writer, lawyer, and civil-rights advocate Michelle Alexander to famously declare mass incarceration to be the "new Jim Crow." And it's what keeps Toure doing pro bono legal work even though she ostensibly retired from law in 2011, as well as what keeps her committed to removing Confederate symbols. The Forrest statue, Toure explained, was an expression of that system; the system a continuation of the symbol. Same war, same general.

"This is what this culture does. You hear the stories of this unarmed Black man being shot in the back. But the stories every day of young Black men being traumatized, men illegally stopped and searched and accused of crimes, losing their dignity—these are the stories that are never told . . . Until we win that war against these statues of people who laid the foundations of white supremacy," Toure emphasized, her voice rising in anger. "Until we expose and remove them, we will continue to have Black people marginalized in this country."

And so the battle continued. The litigation, too. In 2012, Godwin attempted to bring charges against Toure for stealing wreaths from the cemetery; Toure sued Godwin for calling her a "domestic terrorist."

On September 25, 2012, a group of fifty marched on City Hall to hand-deliver letters decrying the statue and to insist that the council intervene in the construction. The Friends of Forrest had undertaken renovations with the assumption that the Selma chapter of the United Daughters of the Confederacy owned the acre of land in Old Live Oak, per an 1877 agreement between the city council and the Ladies Memorial Association (a predecessor organization to the UDC). Toure's husband, state senator Hank Sanders, argued that because the land transfer was not official, the Circle remained city property and thus within the ken of the city to regulate. Godwin, the UDC, and the Friends of Forrest remained adamant that the land was theirs. What did the deed to the land say? The city attorney couldn't find it. So the city revoked KTK Mining's work permit, "over questions about who owns the circle."

But pulling the permit only muddied things further. Because the city council failed to give KTK Mining proper notice that they were deliberating on their work permit, it had thus denied them the opportunity to be heard on the matter. KTK Mining sued the city for violating their due process. It was, of all things, a Fourteenth Amendment issue in federal court that would decide Forrest's fate.

In the meantime, police had managed to unlock Spicer's phone and access its data. They found no footage of the statue's theft. I found an email posted to a Confederate message board, purportedly from Pat Godwin, in which she updated her followers on the investigation, leaving no question about the dehumanizing nature of the statue replacement campaign:

Obviously, "somebody" must've tipped her off when the detectives left for Montgomery to seize her phone… sooooooo, she gave them "A phone".…. not necessarily "the phone"!!!! Guess ole Sherrette is smarter than the average monkey! The informants have been questioned again recently and they stand by their statement that they saw Sherrette Spicer holding the NBF bust AFTER it was taken from the cemetery.…I smell a rat in Zimbabwe on de Alabamy!

FOUR

Deo Vindice

It's no surprise that a decision on the ownership of Confederate Memorial Circle languished in federal court for over a year, because the one-acre plot has long been a proxy battle for the meaning of America's past. Just a few rows up from Confederate Memorial Circle stands a statue of Elodie Todd Dawson. In contrapposto and a flowing gown, she holds a wreath in one hand, a Bible in the other. Her expression is ruminative, not quite serene. It was Dawson's wish to be buried close to Confederate Memorial Circle, her postbellum passion project.

During the American Revolution, New Yorkers took down the statue of King George. After World War Two, Allied troops diligently removed Nazi symbolism from occupied Germany. After the Battle of Baghdad in 2003, American Marines toppled the statue of Saddam Hussein. But after the American Civil War, statues of the losers started to go up instead. Why? Elodie Todd Dawson's work on Confederate Memorial Circle offers an answer.

After the war, Elodie Todd Dawson, like so many women in the South, took up the burden of carrying on. Death had come for one in five Confederate soldiers and for all three of Elodie's brothers: one at Shiloh, one at Vicksburg, one outside Baton Rouge. Her sister Emilie lost her husband to a bullet at Chickamauga;

sister Mary lost hers to a bullet at Ford's Theater in the nation's capital. Husband Nathaniel made it home to Elodie and to their two-year-old son, but war tempered his ego; the emancipation of the fifty-three men and women they enslaved shrank his fortune. He wrote in a letter of "[h]ow little we should value public applause . . . It is [as evaporative] as water and the longer I live the less inclined I am to be influenced by it."

But Elodie's grief moved outward. She sought to make sense of the loss by enlisting as a foot soldier for the Lost Cause, the campaign of revisionist history that glorified the Confederate soldier as a gallant knight who fought to protect his unimpeachable Southern way of life. By emphasizing the valor of the soldier, the tragedy of his death, white Southerners sidestepped the thornier questions of slavery and white supremacy as the Confederacy's raison d'être.

Instead, cemeteries like Old Live Oak became ground zero for the magical thinking of the Lost Cause advocates, who emphasized the fact of the fighting, not its purpose or its consequence. Elodie Dawson became the first president of the Ladies Memorial Association in Selma. She requested and was granted an acre of land from Selma's all-white city council and duly established the Confederate Memorial Circle. It was her dying wish to be buried in sight of the Circle. Nathaniel obliged: He sent for seventy live oaks from Mobile and sent to Italy for a statue of her with a chain of flowers around her neck, a Bible in her hands. When it came in 1879, Dawson sent it back: The curls did not do his late wife justice.

And Elodie Todd Dawson was not alone in her eagerness to find GRANDEUR IN GRAVES, as the inscription on a pillar in Confederate Memorial Circle reads. In his book *Race and Reunion*, David Blight reads the Reconstruction era as, "The story of how the American culture of romance triumphed over reality, sentimental remembrance won over ideological memory." Groups such as hers captained the campaign to refer to the war as the "war between the States." They wrote textbook curricula, sponsored essay contests, and erected monuments to the fallen Confederate soldier. As Blight writes, "In all their efforts the UDC planted a white supremacist vision of the Lost Cause deeper into the nation's historical imagination than perhaps any other association." To borrow George Orwell's formula, the UDC's success at controlling the past meant they controlled the future: now our present. The war might have led to Emancipation, but the narrative of racial difference used to justify slavery carried on. Mary Singleton Slack, a UDC leader in Kentucky, said in a Decoration Day speech in 1904, "thought is power" and urged the UDC to build "the greatest of all monuments, a thought monument."

And they succeeded. So when the student teacher in my ninth-grade history class launched the Civil War unit with the claim that the war was fought over states' rights, he rode a ripple cast by Elodie Todd Dawson's stone up to Central Pennsylvania to hoist one more thought monument.

But Old Live Oak also holds a counternarrative to Selma's Reconstruction, though its marker lay buried and obscured until the mid-1980s. It's the story of Benjamin Turner, born into slavery near Weldon, North Carolina, in 1825. Five years later, his master, Elizabeth Turner, a widow, left Weldon for Selma. Benjamin Turner came of age in the city, and covertly learned to read and write by following the education of Turner's children. In 1845, Elizabeth Turner sold control of him to W. H. Gee, a hotel and stable owner. Turner managed both for Gee, who gave him a meager portion of the profits, which he saved. After the war, Turner bought a parcel of land, taught in the first Freedmen's School, and served as the Dallas County tax collector in 1867.

Selma lay in the third of five military districts in the South, occupied by federal troops overseeing the Southern states' reentry to the Union during Reconstruction. Major J. B. Houston, provost marshal of the Selma Freedmen's Bureau—the underfunded, overstretched federal program that oversaw everything from education to voting rights for those formerly enslaved living in the South—reported more than ten instances of white on Black violence in August 1865 alone, while noting that these events were "but a small part of those that have actually been perpetrated." Between the end of Reconstruction and the outbreak of World War II, nineteen racial terror lynchings would take place in Dallas County, one of the highest totals of the Jim Crow era. Yet the formerly enslaved persisted, organized, and asserted their rights. Having decided that the education being provided by white Northerners was not up to par, Turner helped to organize and found the Freedmen's School, in the basement of First Baptist Church on Selma's East End. Such institutions became, as Dr. Carroll Van West notes in his survey of Selma's historic places, "the first steps to asserting their place not only within the society but also within the actual physical landscape of the town."

In 1870, Turner was elected to the House of Representatives, representing Alabama's First District as the first Black Alabamian in

Congress. You can see him in a famous lithograph made by Currier and Ives that depicts seven newly elected Black congressmen—he's second from the left, with a full beard and a stern expression. While in Washington, Turner advocated for reparations and for desegregated schools—one of the first to do so in the US Congress. But he also advocated for leniency toward former Confederates, to restore their legal and political rights. Congress ignored all three proposed bills (though the next Congress would reenfranchise all former Confederates who took an oath of loyalty to the Union). Turner, however, did manage to secure legislation giving military pensions to Black soldiers.

That lithograph is a stirring reminder that it didn't have to be this way. That America could have been a different country and that, briefly, we were. During those few years after the war, the country actively vested and protected the citizenship of Black Americans. The Thirteenth, Fourteenth, and Fifteenth Amendments were passed, Black officials elected, and a pluralistic society—rather than one predicated on white supremacy—seemed possible.

Instead, Turner lost the Republican primary election in 1872, and the last of his colleagues in that lithograph left office in 1877. The next Black congressman from Alabama wouldn't take office for another century. Turner returned to Selma and to farming, but lost his business to the down economy at the end of the decade. Though he served as an election official throughout the two decades after leaving Congress, he died penniless on his farm outside Selma in 1894.

Nathaniel Dawson had written often of his hope that having married a Todd sister would "save me the trouble of being hanged," but Reconstruction went much easier on former Confederates than Dawson anticipated. In the late 1860s and early 1870s, local dens of the Ku Klux Klan, helmed by their Grand Wizard Nathan Bedford Forrest in Memphis, targeted prominent freedmen and Republicans with vigilante violence and intimidation in an effort to deliver the South back to Democratic, white-supremacist rule. "From 1866 through 1871, men calling themselves 'Ku-Klux' killed hundreds of Black Southerners and their white supporters, sexually molested hundreds of Black women and men, drove thousands of Black families from their homes and thousands of Black men and women from their employment, and appropriated land, crops, guns, livestock, and food from Black Southerners on a massive scale," Elaine Frantz Parsons writes in her early history of the Klan. With white power restored and with no gallows to fret over, Dawson headed north to serve as President Grover Cleveland's Commissioner of the Bureau of Education.

In 1901, seven years after Turner's death, Alabamians gathered in Constitutional convention, their explicit purpose, as convention president John Knox put it: "To establish white supremacy in this state. This is our problem, and we should be permitted to deal with it, unobstructed by outside influences." Votes to ratify the new constitution were close in all counties but the Black Belt, which, oddly, voted overwhelmingly for it, suggesting to some historians that either the counties fixed the vote or perhaps refused to hold an election at all. The new constitution imposed poll taxes, property requirements, tests of literacy and constitutional knowledge, and other barriers to the franchise, which dropped the statewide number of Black registered voters from more than 180,000 to less than 4,000, and in Dallas county, from

9,871 to 152—the latter a number that hardly wavered until the passage of the Voting Rights Act more than sixty years later. Such tests, of course, might have disqualified poor illiterate white Alabamians if not for a clause that permitted those descendants of veterans to register. Deo Vindice, indeed.

In the mid-1980s, Selma historian Alston Fitts identified Turner's grave in Old Live Oak and worked to raise funds for a proper monument for Alabama's first Black congressman. He recalled the pushback he faced during his campaign to publicly commemorate Turner, telling me that when he mentioned the project to a member of the Chamber of Commerce, she responded, "We try and focus on the more positive aspects of Selma history."

"Oh, like what?" he asked.

"Like when the Yankees burned the town."

FIVE

From Civil War to Civil Rights

In October of 2013, US District Judge Kristi Dubose ruled in favor of KTK Mining and ordered the city to settle with the group. To resolve the issue, as per Judge Dubose's ruling, the City Council would first have to decide who owned the land before they could decide what might happen on it. A month later, the council proposed terms. Arguing that it would be cheaper in the long run to settle, they proposed to deed the acre to the UDC and pay KTK Mining $100,000—a third of the amount for which they had sued. Further: the Friends of Forrest could replace the bust, but it could not be further elevated or illuminated. Three times Toure tried to speak and three times she was told she was out of order. Finally, council president Corey Bowie had her removed and arrested, and Toure spent the night in the Dallas County jail.

At a council meeting the following January, ahead of the vote to finalize the agreement and officially deed the acre to the UDC, a group of activists including Toure began singing in the chamber. Police removed the protesters. From the lobby they sang and chanted and beat the doors as the council voted 5–4 in favor of the agreement.

But Sherrette Spicer stayed behind. "Rosa Park-ing on their ass," as she described it to me.

When Spicer started to tell me this story, she paused, then backed up: "Let me set the scene for you." But instead of describing the atmosphere in the room, the under-the-breath side conversations of the activists about to march out, or what was going through her head as she prepared to do whatever she was about to do, she described for me the city's logo, which hung behind the city councilors. "From Civil War to Civil Rights and Beyond," its motto reads, circling an image of the Edmund Pettus Bridge and a Greek-revival mansion.

Then Spicer stood.

"You're fired," she yelled as she approached the front of the room.

As the *Selma Times-Journal* reported, "Spicer ran behind the council's desk and yelled into the audience, likening the decision to the Ku Klux Klan." She threw down chairs and tables to block city police from reaching her before she could get to the podium and say to their faces that they need to revote.

"Shame on you," she called as police tackled her on the steps leading up to the councilors' seats.

So: from the Civil War to civil rights and beyond. "We ain't got to the beyond yet," Spicer explained.

Spicer's story brought a line from Alston Fitts to mind again, about how Selma had more history than it knew what to do with. I realized, though, listening to Spicer's story, that it was less about having too much history and more about coming to terms with the consequences of it—a task that Selma, like the country at large, struggles to do.

After the council's vote, the Friends of Forrest got back to work. A year later, with more history than we know what to do with, I first wandered into Confederate Memorial Circle on the fiftieth anniversary of Bloody Sunday. Soon after, Forrest came around again, followed then by Dylann Roof.

IN THE INVITATION to the replacement statue's unveiling, Pat Godwin wrote, "This will be a HUGE MONUMENTAL HISTORICAL event—the most paramount Confederate accomplishment throughout the South in recent times because we beat the enemy in their own territory, the Civil Rights hotspot of the world!" Though most white people have left Selma, its status as a symbolic city—"enemy territory" as Godwin put it—remains, not despite the white flight, but because of it. With the bust, the Friends of Forrest laid siege on the symbolic city from afar. They no longer want to live there, but still want to exert power over it, control its history.

And with the circle secured, they wanted to hold on to the story, too. Todd Kiscaden never returned my phone calls. Cecil Williamson, a board member of the Friends of Forrest and a city council member during the debates in 2012, likewise let his phone ring. When I stopped by the auto-body shop run by Benny Austin, the spokesman for the Friends of Forrest, he told me that he wasn't going to talk to me, that he wasn't going to open that scab. "But you put the statue up," I started to say, but he had already retreated to the back of the shop. I spoke with Pat Godwin several times on the phone and each time arranged for an in-person interview, only for her to cancel at the last minute. Finally, she wrote to say that she had discussed the matter with the Friends of Forrest board and they'd decided that they "won't give interviews toward a project that we would have no control over the finished product." She was sorry, she said, but she thought it best "for the integrity of 'our' own story." Deo vindice, I guess.

A FEW MONTHS after the statue's rededication, in the summer of 2015, I headed to Selma to see the new Forrest bust for the first time. The granite pedestal was taller than I'd remembered, its base coming almost to my head (though its seeming taller may have had something to do with the fact that there was now a bust on top). Anyway, it looms. Looking at the statue from a few feet away—with the requisite, if only slight, crane of your neck to meet the statue's gaze—forces you into a position of fealty, which I suppose is the point. It was evening, the waning light diffuse behind low cloud cover, casting no shadow. Everything was saturated—matte and flat and color-true. It's the kind of light I've only seen in the American southeast; the kind of light that makes William Eggleston's photographs so distinct—doleful and arresting. The dark bronze whorls of Forrest's face glowed, almost. Up close, I could see the reproduction of Forrest's signature carved under his general's jacket. I resisted the urge to touch the points of his slicked-back hair, to see if they were sharp.

I was out there that evening in a Confederate cemetery because I had decided to use these Forrest monuments as a way of organizing the past, to make sense of the present, and as it was becoming clear, to make sense of myself. I was there because there isn't a Forrest statue in, say, Lancaster—just the burnt pylons in the Susquehanna that let me think I had avoided being implicated. And I admit that when I started coming to Selma, I thought of the city in terms not so far from what Vaughan Russell described as the folks who come to kiss the Blarney Stone. The city existed for me as it does in the national imagination as "Selma," a repository of violence and grainy history. But I've since come to think of it more as a stage for America's dramas and anxieties.

Generals Wilson and Forrest came to Selma in 1865 because the city was a major arsenal of the Confederacy. It equipped the defense of the institution that enslaved people to work the surrounding farmland in order to line the nation's pockets, from Selma's Commercial Bank of Alabama to the textile mills of Massachusetts. One hundred years after Forrest lost the first battle of Selma, Dr. King chose the city as a place to stage the civil rights movement's campaign for voting rights because it had so thoroughly rejected the outcome of the Civil War and could thus dramatize in stark terms the consequences, paid by the country at large, of our larger national rejection of that outcome. Spoiling for a second battle of Selma, the city's white people violently defended a white power structure that existed, albeit in less stark terms, throughout the country. The violence on the Edmund Pettus Bridge provided the political theater necessary to pass *federal* legislation, after all. Selma's 1990 school resegregation was particularly dramatic, yes, but school integration efforts in the United States peaked in 1988. Then white folks beat the dusty trail to suburbs the country over. Likewise, it is hard to survey the backlash to James Perkins, Jr.'s election, from the vantage point of the present day, without feeling like it presaged the nation's reaction to Obama's presidency. And Selma, in its battle over a Confederate monument, once more served as a bellwether. Selma's stories are more American than we often like to think—more representative than aberrant.

So Selma hasn't gone from the Civil War to civil rights and beyond, but, really, where in America have we? The lie of racial difference that was used to justify slavery persisted long after its abolition. After the war, embodiments of the lie emerged in the North as well as the South: lynching, red-lining, mass incarceration, to name just a few. And the legislative victories of the civil rights movement could only partially address a lie so pernicious and persistent. Lerone Bennett, Jr., writing under a banner image of sneering sheriff's deputies in Selma in *Ebony*'s August 1965 issue, reminds us that "There is no Negro problem. The problem of race in America, insofar as that problem is related to packets of melanin in men's skins, is a white problem." And it is a problem that persists. The "beyond" remains a mythical place where the color of your skin is not the predictor of so many outcomes, from health, wealth, opportunity, and prison time.

Still, a Forrest statue lost and found in the city that Pat Godwin calls the "Civil rights hotspot" makes the country's unreconciled tension more visible. Reencountering American history through Selma's prism is to see it in that evening's light—stark, diffuse, the saturation turned way way up. So there I was, in the gloaming of one of the year's longest days, staring into the bronze eyes of an ersatz Forrest bust, seeing not one city's talisman to the unreconstructed, but rather the whole tragic farce of America's sense, my own sense of history. Then I got back in my dusty old sedan and set off to chronicle the battles that Selma precipitated—the new fronts in the cold Civil War.

PART TWO

Forrest in the Age of Confederate Reproduction

Murfreesboro

SIX

Laying Forrest Low

They built the coffin from cardboard, the body from papier-mâché, and at noon on a clear and cold November day, students at Middle Tennessee State University in Murfreesboro, Tennessee, buried Nathan Bedford Forrest in effigy. On the lawn of the squat, two-story brick building, unremarkable save for the fact that it bears the general's name, the group circled, held hands, and laid the body down.

"It's 2015," one attendee said. "It's time to bury him."

The group had marched from the student union, a half-mile across the sprawling campus, to the impromptu burial ground in front of Forrest Hall, the university's ROTC building. Two students, serving as pallbearers, carried the black cardboard coffin. Inside was the papier-mâché cast of the general, wearing a gray Confederate jacket and a Ku Klux Klan hood.

As they marched, they chanted:

"Run, Forrest, run!"

"Black lives matter!"

"Change that name!"

"It was a really brave, smart thing to do," Elizabeth Catte, then a Ph.D. candidate in public history at MTSU, told me. Forrest Hall is in the middle of the 22,000-person campus, a stone's throw from the registrar's office and the on-campus Subway. The burial raised the stakes in a campaign started that summer to change the name of MTSU's Forrest Hall, and was meant to galvanize support on campus. At the front of the march was Joshua Crutchfield, one of the leaders of the campaign. Crutchfield was then a masters candidate in history, studying activism in the Black church. Bookish and bearded, Crutchfield is a natural organizer, combining a deep knowledge of both history and political organizing with a contagious charisma.

When the march reached the lawn of Forrest Hall, Dalton Winfree, an MTSU senior with glasses, a scruffy beard, and a flop of hair, opened the coffin and removed the puppetlike effigy. "Today we are having a burial of Nathan Bedford Forrest," Winfree announced, "to send a message to the task force who refuses to acknowledge his racist past."

The task force to which Winfree referred had been convened by the school's president, Sidney McPhee, to determine the appropriateness of the ROTC hall's name. Derek Frisby, a global studies professor specializing in military history, would lead a group of sixteen students, faculty, alumni, and community members to debate and then recommend to President McPhee whether the university should change the name, leave the name alone, or leave the name with "added historical context." McPhee had announced the task force back in August, in response to on-campus protests in the aftermath of the Charleston Nine murders, when students, professors, and community members demanded the university remove the name that they felt most clearly represented white supremacy.

That fall, similar campaigns were being launched at campuses across the country. Students, from Southern state schools to Northern Ivies, were holding their administrators to account for their statues, symbols, and building names—taking such honorifics as indications of who belonged, whose histories were remembered, whose lives mattered. The murders in Charleston had sensitized many students to the values reflected by their campus landscape, and they found that American universities had much with which to reckon: histories of owning and selling enslaved people; campuses built with slave labor; buildings named for the intellectual defenders of slavery; active, and in many cases violent, resistance to integration; campus cultures still hostile to students of color. At Yale, this meant a campaign to rename Calhoun College—the residence hall named for John Calhoun, known as the intellectual architect of the Confederacy. At the University of North Carolina, this triggered protests to remove "Silent Sam"—an on-campus statue of a Confederate soldier. At the University of Missouri, this meant a campus-wide outcry over the administration's tepid response to racist incidents on campus that included racial slurs smeared in feces on bathroom walls, leading a graduate student to stage a hunger strike and the football team to threaten to sit out upcoming games.

And, at MTSU, this meant a reckoning with Forrest.

Many in Murfreesboro see Forrest as their savior. This owes to a raid Forrest led in the summer of 1862, driving out Union occupiers from the town, saving several men from imminent execution, and returning the city to Confederate control (at least for five months, anyway, until the Battle of Stones River, a bloody affair in which the Union retook the city). Southern novelist and critic Andrew Lytle, in an admiring biography, dubs Forrest "the town's deliverer." And, as legend has it, a descendent of one of the men Forrest saved later donated land to the university. So, the Confederate logic went, no Forrest, no Middle Tennessee State.

MTSU, a public university, is now the state's second largest school, known for its audio production program, and students of color make up a third of the student body. But for almost as long as MTSU has been a school, it has been tangled up in Forrest. At various points in the school's history, Forrest has appeared in bronze on the front of the student union, in ink and on horseback at the top of the school's stationery, embodied as a mascot on the sidelines of the football field; and, as the Dean of Students Belt Keathley said when dedicating Forrest Hall in 1958, his spirit has always been close at hand. This adoration helps explain why, 138 years after he was first laid to rest in Memphis's Elmwood Cemetery, it was necessary now to bury Forrest in effigy. Decades of protests led by students of color had gradually forced the university to shed most of its Forrest emblems. The 2015–2016 campaign took aim at his last symbolic outpost: Forrest Hall.

The task force had until that April to make their recommendation, but should the group endorse a name change, it would only be the first handoff in a much longer relay. President McPhee would take that decision under consideration and, should he agree, he would then make his recommendation to the Tennessee Board of Regents, who oversee Middle Tennessee State. Then, should the Board of Regents likewise concur that the name should be changed, they would have to appeal to the Tennessee Historical Commission for approval to rechristen the ROTC building. That last procedural hurdle would come from the Tennessee Heritage Protection Act, passed in 2013, which requires the state's historical commission to sign off on any change to monuments on public property. The Heritage Protection Act (sometimes jokingly referred to by journalists in the state as the Nathan Bedford Forrest Protection Act) was passed as a rearguard response to the decision by the city of Memphis to rename Forrest Park earlier that year. Confederate memory was well fortified. State senator Bill Ketron (Republican, Murfreesboro; MTSU '83) sponsored the Heritage Protection Act and would serve on the Forrest Hall task force. The first public forum would convene two weeks after the symbolic funeral; the task force would hear from all comers.

The ensuing debate over Forrest's life and legacy would turn on the same questions that were currently roiling schools and cities across the country: questions about racial equity, about whose memory matters, about what our symbols say about who we are and what we need. And the debates over these questions would reveal a deep rift in American life. As a prelude to this battle, the students laid his papier-mâché body low. Holding hands in a ring around the coffin, the protesters sang and chanted. When they dispersed, they left the body on the stoop of his hall.

SEVEN

We Have a Choice

When I met Joshua Crutchfield to discuss his role in the campaign to rename Forrest Hall, he wore thick-framed glasses, an easy smile, and because he'd just come from helping his cousin move, stylish athleisure wear. Crutchfield grew up in Murfreesboro and still has family close by. He is the cofounder of the #blcktwitterstorians, a popular hashtag for activists and historians of color, and he speaks in a measured cadence that belies his spirited, and at times confrontational, organizing style. He told me that he wanted to take on Forrest because he wanted MTSU to be better, more equitable, and more accountable to its past—and because he has borne the weight of its failure to do so.

"Bree Newsome was the spark for me," he explained. The community organizer and activist who climbed the flagpole of the South Carolina Capitol to remove the Confederate flag two weeks after the Charleston Nine shooting made Crutchfield think the timing was right to get Forrest's name taken down, too. He'd cut his teeth organizing with the Black Lives Matter chapter in Nashville and, in the summer of 2015, saw a potential opportunity for a groundswell of protests to rename the building at MTSU. "There's always a small group of people holding things together until something big happens and you can draw more people to your effort," Crutchfield explained. So he and a few other MTSU students began to organize a movement to change the name. They soon started a Facebook page and circulated a petition. It got upward of one thousand signatures in the first week. After the group's first public protest that August, the school president, Dr. McPhee, announced that he would convene the task force.

But the timeline and format of the process frustrated Crutchfield, who felt the matter was cut and dry: "We don't think racism should be debated at this point," he said. "We shouldn't have to beg to be acknowledged or cared for." The drawn-out format seemed intentional, an attempt to slow the campaign's momentum. But, he felt, it also created a false equivalency—the equal time, "hear-both-sides" format suggesting that Forrest's military accomplishments should be considered equal to his actions as a slave-trader and a Klansman. It was, in a word, "bullshit." But even so, he said, "We committed to the process." Crutchfield and his fellow organizers came up with a two-pronged strategy for how they would engage the deliberations. "If you participate in the meetings, you legitimize it. If you disrupt it, you say it's bullshit," he explained. They decided to do both.

THE FIRST FORUM took place in December, a few weeks after the papier-mâché Forrest's funeral, and the "Change the Name" group came out en masse, ready to participate in the spirit of the forums. The night was organized in a point–counterpoint format: People wishing to speak in favor of the name change could sign up in one column, those wishing to keep the name, in the other. Two minutes were allotted for a speaker wanting to keep the name, then two minutes for someone wanting it to change. Unsurprisingly, the atmosphere was tense.

"There was lots of silence before the proceedings," Mark Doyle, an MTSU history professor and member of the task force, told me, with "people eyeing each other nervously." He likened the mood to a Trump rally.

"The pro- and anti-Forrest camps break down predictably," Doyle explained.

The "Change the Name" coalition consisted primarily of students—mostly students of color, but not exclusively so—with the additional participation of some professors and community members. Their appeals worked past and present. They hit the big three strikes against Forrest: slaver, Fort Pillow massacre, KKK. They weren't trying to change history, they noted, which resides in the historical record. The question of honoring someone, however, is a different matter entirely. Heaping laurels on a man with Forrest's record simply didn't square with a public university claiming inclusivity.

And white Southern history was not, in fact, the only history to consider.

"When I see him I see what my enslaved ancestors went through," one student testified.

Crutchfield spoke toward the end of the first meeting and threw down the gauntlet: "We have a choice: Do Black lives matter or will we hold on to white supremacy?"

Those in the pro-Forrest camp were mostly white, mostly older, mostly from the Murfreesboro community, not the university—representatives of the so-called Buckle of the Bible Belt. Their arguments outlined their fear of changing history, the history of their ancestors, whose heritage they valued. They recited the doctrine of Forrest apologia: That he was a daring commander; that he displayed admirable leadership qualities; that he was as a man of his time, a time when slavery was legal. Some testified that his presence on campus reflected their values and represented the community's connection to the school. Former ROTC cadets fondly remembered rappelling off the building named for the general. Then, of course, there was the more general anti-political correctness debate that reliably attends such discussions. Don't judge a historical figure by today's PC standards, the line went. As one speaker put it: "I'm offended that you're offended."

Elizabeth Coker, a local journalist and the proprietor of Nostalgic Nashville, a tour guide to Old South points of interest, testified that members of her family rode with Forrest and she refused to see that history diminished. When I spoke with Coker after the forums, she framed the debate as one of "town vs. gown"—a tension between MTSU and the local population. The university is changing. No longer a regional school, MTSU attracts a diverse group of students from across the state and across the country. That's evidence to some that Forrest needs to go. But to others, the changing campus makes it more urgent that Forrest stay. Forrest, as Coker explained, represented a link to the past, to their past. Who were these outsiders to tell them otherwise? "I feel it is an intrusion on our culture and on our perspective on life," Coker told me.

Those wanting to change the name, she felt, did not understand General Forrest. Nor did they understand the connection, the respect, that people there feel for him. "It goes back so far into the school's psyche," she explained. It was all so personal. To protest Forrest, the town savior, was a protest against their home and history. In other words, a protest against *them*. "The younger generation has skipped all that history and just moved on to social justice." And social justice, for Elizabeth Coker, wasn't the point. Take white privilege, she said. "My grandmother had no concept about that during the Great Depression and I don't think I ever have either, but I will say that I'm a very blessed person and I haven't suffered near what generations before me has." She pointed to the English and Irish settlers in Middle Tennessee fleeing persecution in Europe, then to the white Southerners after the war, facing starvation and the destruction of their land and the upheaval of their society, then to the deprivation of the Great Depression. Life hasn't been easy on her people, she feels, and then here come these social-justice kids begrudging her her heroes? She wouldn't stand for it. Forrest—Tennessee's legendary soldier, in her estimation—was worth defending, regardless of the outcome (or the meaning) of the war he fought. "Losers in history are not necessarily losers. You might lose the battle and you might even lose the war. But history usually will bear out the truth of what was a righteous cause."

FOR THE SECOND forum, held in February 2016 at a community center west of campus, the "Change the Name" group revised their approach. Sheriff's deputies, there for security at the off-campus event, stood along the walls, hands on hips and holsters. There were reports of intimidation in the crowd. Pat Godwin made the trip up I-65 from Selma to speak, calling attention to the thousands of Mexicans crossing the US southern border while they were there, wringing hands about political correctness.

An hour into the forum, Brandon Woodruff took the microphone. Woodruff, that year's homecoming king and a member of a group of Black student leaders known as the Talented Tenth, wore a white turtleneck sweater and a look of firm resolve. An alumni speaking a few turns before Woodruff had threatened to pull his donation from the school should they change the name. Woodruff promised much worse: a third of the student body— the approximate percentage of students of color on campus— rising up against the administration in revolt. The administration, Woodruff said, had consistently overlooked and ignored the experiences of people of color, but they would not be ignored any longer. "We will fight until hell freezes over," he said, "and then we will fight on the ice."

He replaced the microphone in the stand, took his seat, and joined a crowd of students in a chant of "Change the damn name!"

Then Crutchfield stepped into the aisle and led a group of students in a recitation of Assata Shakur's rallying call: "It is our duty to fight for our freedom. It is our duty to win. We must love and support each other. We have nothing to lose but our chains." A sheriff's deputy then shepherded him out of the room, to the chants of "Black lives matter." A dozen more students followed, heading for the center aisle, their fists raised, pumping their arms with every syllable. People stiffened in their chairs. The forum ground to a halt. A deputy approached Derek Frisby, the chair of the task force, wanting to end the event then and there, but Frisby declined. They waited. The students' muffled chants filtered into the room. People exchanged hesitant looks, coughed, fidgeted. Finally, the meeting resumed, but the tenor had changed. The seats once occupied by the students remained conspicuously empty.

I spoke with Dr. Frisby a few months after the task force had made their final recommendation. Frisby wore the familiar uniform of a college professor: light-blue button-down shirt, khakis, high-mileage sneakers. On his bookshelf stood figurine soldiers squared off in miniature battle. During our conversation, Frisby described what it was like to chair a conversation on one of America's oldest unresolved arguments. "There's no way to talk about Forrest objectively," he told me, he was just too controversial. He conceded that maybe there could have been a better way to organize the forums than the "tit-for-tat" format but, even after many sleepless nights, he hadn't thought of one. Forrest was a historical trip wire pulled tight by the tensions of the present, and for Frisby the forums became a microcosm of a broader us-versus-them political climate. "Everyone was already polarized," he explained. In his view, both camps thought the debate was preposterous, the answer was obvious, and the process was rigged against them.

Like Elizabeth Coker, Dr. Frisby pointed to a generational gap to account for the divide. Frisby had grown up in Murfreesboro, attended MTSU, and teaches in Forrest Hall. He saw the decision to name the building after Forrest as an attempt to connect the school to the community. And he appreciated the gesture. But, he acknowledged, the school has changed, that connection has frayed, and he allowed that there were figures other than Forrest the school might honor. Still, he had hoped that the debate would be a learning experience for the students.

Instead, it only wore on them, Joshua Crutchfield told me. The debates and forums and online arguments drained them physically and emotionally. Because the school's administration had tried to carve out a neutral stance on Forrest, the burden of outlining his full history and testifying to the dehumanizing effects of it fell to the students, who were told repeatedly, on their own campus, that they were dumb, that they were wasting their time, that if only they knew their history, they would come to admire the man. It seemed to Crutchfield that the students were working harder to better the school than the school was to better them. He found those months of debate depressing, heavy. They were asking members of their community to acknowledge a point of view outside their own, and for it they were mocked. The county historian, Greg Tucker, even wrote a letter in support of keeping the name, claiming that the students, in making this debate about race, were letting Martin Luther King down.

One of the members of the task force, history professor Mark Doyle, decried this pushback in an open letter. Titled "To the White People Who Publicly Opposed the Renaming of MTSU's Nathan Bedford Forrest Hall," Doyle diagnosed a misguided belief in "The True History." He wrote: "You feared that the True History of Nathan Bedford Forrest was being distorted or hijacked by people without a valid claim to the story, such as you have. Newcomers and dilettantes were grabbing the Facts of History and twisting them to their own selfish purposes." He invited his readers to consider the fact that students like Crutchfield "were saying that your True History is not a divinely sanctioned absolute, but simply a story about the past that helps you make sense of the present, and that this, far from being a perversion of history, is what history actually is." Those who want to change the name, he wrote, "are people who resent white people continuing to claim ownership of their stories, their bodies, and the manner in which they engage with the world as they find it."

After that second forum, Crutchfield returned home exhausted. But, ever the student of history, he unwound by reading. He'd come across a new article published by an author he admired, the historian Robin D.G. Kelley. The article questioned university protests led by Black students across the country. "I want to think about what it means for Black students to seek love from an institution incapable of loving them," Kelley writes in the essay. It was like Kelley was writing directly to Crutchfield. Given the systemic prejudice the students were protesting, Kelley asked, why demand more access to such institutions? The article forced Crutchfield to rethink his motivation. What was he fighting for? he asked himself. At what table was he trying to get a seat? Did he even want to be at that table?

Crutchfield told me about how stressful it was to be a student of color at MTSU, Forrest protests aside. He talked about having been the only Black student in his masters' cohort, about the condescending feedback he would get on his work; about how other students, in subsequent cohorts, would talk about the same stressors. Still, he acknowledged how much the school has contributed to his growth, how influential some of the professors have been on his thinking. "It's kind of like living in America," he explains. "You care for it, but how much energy do I put toward making a place change that historically hasn't cared for me?"

Maybe the fatigue Crutchfield was feeling was intergenerational. "For as long as Black students have been on campus," Crutchfield lamented, "they have been protesting this."

EIGHT

The Marshmallow Wonderland
of the Past

Nearly fifty years before Crutchfield marched on Forrest Hall, Sylvester Brooks went to the only Middle Tennessee State football game he'd attend, as a student there in the late sixties. Brooks, a tall seventeen-year-old with short-cropped hair and sideburns, arrived on campus in the fall of 1967 in one of the earliest integrated MTSU classes. A few months into his time at MTSU, the university raised an eight-foot, six-hundred-pound bronze medallion of Forrest on the front of the student center. Brooks's first dorm room was a repurposed storage closet, windowless and cramped. It took his roommate's sustained complaints to get them reassigned to a proper room. Between classes, white students would come up to him and ask to touch his hair and skin; others, who had grown up in the hills of east Tennessee, were seeing a Black person for the first time when they walked past him on the quad.

"It did make you feel like you were in *The Twilight Zone*, that there were people walking around on this earth that were at that level," Brooks said in an oral history conducted by MTSU in 2000. "How can we talk about the issues that I want to talk about when people are wondering how my hair feels?"

Brooks had a sense of the racial tension he would encounter at MTSU. A politically active teenager who attended a segregated high school in Memphis, he actively sought to confront (and, he hoped, begin to ameliorate) white people's pathologies about race in an integrated space. And, since it was up to him to create that integrated space, he enrolled at MTSU—an integrated school with a good prelaw program.

So Brooks headed out to Floyd Stadium one Saturday in 1968 with trepidation. As an incoming student, he'd been given a campus tour by a Black upperclassman, who, Brooks remembered, told him that going to a game would be a "unique experience." Still, he wanted to see it for himself. As he looked up into the bleachers that day, here's what he saw: the student section, white faces all, flapping Confederate flags in the autumn breeze. The flag had been a mainstay at MTSU games for years. The previous spring's yearbook included a photo of white students holding the stars and bars, captioned with this: "HAPPINESS IS having your own Confederate flag to wave at the pep rally." One group of frat brothers would send pledges to games wearing vests of patched-together Confederate flags. Between snaps, the band played "Dixie"—the 1850s minstrel song claimed as the Confederate anthem. Their mascot? A student dressed up as Forrest in a gray wool duster, patrolling the sidelines on horseback.

He wasn't surprised at what he found—he'd been warned, after all—but still, he explained to me, he was shocked. "They had no love for me," he said. Having marched in Memphis and Mississippi as a high school student, Brooks had seen plenty of Confederate flags waved in his direction and harbored no illusions about what those had meant. "They weren't carrying it as we went by talking about their heritage. They were making a point to me about what they thought I was." Back in Memphis, Brooks had even received a menacing letter from someone claiming to be in the Klan. His mother had kept a scrapbook of clippings from Brooks's activism and he texted me a photo of the letter, which warns: "We know how to handle people like you and your kind of filth." But something about the atmosphere in the stands, the glee that so many of his classmates took in this Old South nostalgia, irked him in a different way. "It was more 'in your face,'" Brooks told me. And so, he resolved to challenge it.

THE UNIVERSITY'S SPORTS teams, in its early years, had no official nickname but were known colloquially (and not altogether reverently) as the Teachers or the Pedagogues. And they performed as one might expect a team so named to perform, so in 1934, the local *Daily News Journal* sponsored a contest to renickname the school. A football player, taking inspiration from the Colgate University Red Raiders, suggested the Blue Raiders. For his trouble, the paper gave him $5, and the college took the Blue Raiders for a name. In 1938, when Q. M. Smith became school president, he sought to put a finer point on the name. Which Raider, exactly, was the school embodying? Why, Forrest, of course, the school's logo and stationery soon announced.

After the Second World War, the university experienced a massive increase in the number of veterans attending under the G.I. Bill, and along with them a crop of fresh-faced boys to be trained to fight the proxy battles of the nascent Cold War. A ROTC program was duly established in 1950. Budding soldiers trained on campus to counter Soviet guerilla tactics, with a few maneuvers inspired by Forrest. But the ROTC program needed a home, so they brick-and-mortared Forrest onto the campus. At the christening in 1958, Dean of Students Belt Keathley explained that, "There was no search for a name for the ROTC building. The name was simply present at hand. The spirit of the man for whom the building is named resides on our campus."

Dr. Frisby, the chair of the Forrest Hall task force, touched on the post-war connection between Forrest and the new ROTC program in an essay he wrote, one intended to ground the current Forrest debate in the history of the school's affiliation. "With the campus and community public memory tied inexorably with their martial heritage," Frisby writes, "Forrest rode boldly into Murfreesboro again."

In the broader context of the political moment, however, it's hard to see such Confederate symbolism only in terms of martial heritage. In the years between the Civil War and the civil rights movement, the Confederate flag was rarely publicly displayed. It only came back into wider circulation with Strom Thurmond's Dixiecrat rebellion in 1948—a splinter group of Southern Democrats who opposed the modest civil rights concessions made by President Harry Truman. Then suddenly the flags were everywhere. John Rankin, a congressman from Mississippi, admitted in 1951 that he had "never seen as many Confederate flags in all my life as I have observed floating here in Washington during the last few months." In 1956, Georgia state representative Denmark Groover put a finer point on its reemergence when he claimed that the state's newly approved flag included Confederate symbolism "mostly out of defiance to federal integration orders." The flags that Sylvester Brooks saw at the football game at Floyd stadium were not there by accident. They were there because he was there.

And with the flags came Confederate monuments. The first wave of monument building came around the turn of the century, the symbolic equivalent of the Jim Crow laws then being enacted. Then, in the years between the Supreme Court's Brown vs. Board of Education decision in 1954 and the assassination of Dr. Martin Luther King, Jr., in 1968, there came another wave, this time with an increased emphasis on school names. Public celebrations of Forrest followed this same trajectory. Once a point of civic pride in Memphis, turnout out for Forrest's birthday dwindled in the forties and early fifties. In 1958, however (the same year MTSU dedicated Forrest Hall), hundreds again filled Forrest Park, a crowd that Nathan's great-granddaughter Mary Forrest Bradley attributed to the "desegregation crisis." Given this wider context, and given the fact that in 1958 MTSU had yet to integrate after the Supreme Court's 1954 decision, you have to squint awfully hard to see only the town's martial heritage in that building's name.

THE SCHOOL DID desegregate in 1962. That same year, a premed student from Connecticut named Dick Schooman became the first to portray Forrest as the school's mascot. I found a photo of Schooman in an old MTSU yearbook. He's goateed and uniformed, his jaw clenched and jutted as he leads a horse by the reins in a homecoming procession. The resemblance was uncanny, as if someone had enhanced and retouched one of the old photos of Forrest I've given over so much time to scrutinizing, then slipped the image into an old yearbook. In fact, when

I saw that photograph, I gasped, so loudly that if anyone in the school's archives had heard it, they would have thought it contrived or exaggerated. But it wasn't Forrest. Sitting there in 2016, I stared into a space-time rift, looking at an image of a 1962 impersonation of the general in 1862.

From the perspective of his admirers, it's only natural that Forrest would prowl the sidelines of a football game. Historian Court Carney sees a cult of masculinity surrounding Forrest. In his essay "Most Man in the World," Carney traces this manly reverence for the general from the UDC, who thought of him as a "manly man, fearless and true," to author Shelby Foote, whose admiration of Forrest gives the essay its title and whose depiction of Forrest in his novel *Shiloh* is one of the warrior phallus incarnate: " . . . [H]acking and slashing, riding them down. His saber looked ten feet long; it flashed and glinted." In Carney's view, Robert E. Lee was emasculated by the surrender at Appomattox and so could not bear all the symbolic weight the defeated but unvanquished white South had to heap upon its generals. Lee's gallant respectability, his aristocratic poise, kept him in the collective memory (and in many a courthouse square), but it only got him so far. Whereas Forrest, especially in the second half of the twentieth century, came to represent an increasingly violent masculinity in which "bloodlust replaced chivalry, malicious violence eclipsed moral courage." If football is a way to channel military impulses, then it was only a matter of time before imitation Forrests started popping up on the sidelines in Middle Tennessee.

But with integration came challenges to the school's Confederate costume play. The winter before Sylvester Brooks's lone visit to Floyd Stadium, Brooks remembered that a fight broke out at an MTSU basketball game when the Forrest mascot patted a Black player on the back. The player took exception to this imitation Forrest laying a hand on him and retaliated with his fist. It's a sort of Fort Sumter of MTSU's symbolic civil war—the first shot across the bow in a campaign that has now stretched out for half a century. Previously, the college could claim to see Forrest's hand only as heroic and admirable, holding the reins of the good old days. By the late sixties, they could no longer do so unchecked. Students of color now insisted their white classmates see that hand as one that held the shackles, the saber, the torch.

That fall, a few weeks after Brooks attended that MTSU football game, he published a letter in the school paper. Titled "What Dixie Means," Brooks wrote: "As long as these remnants of slavery and Black inferiority are allowed to persist on this campus, I will never choose to be a full part of this school." He asked his fellow white students if they'd ever thought about what "Dixie" means to a Black student, if they'd ever cared enough to even try to consider it. He called on the school to understand the full context of their symbols and traditions. Desegregation meant the end of a tradition, he wrote, an immoral tradition. "Other traditions are equally wrong and equally outdated. It is time we, as citizens and students, started living in the concrete reality of the present, instead of the marshmellow [sic] wonderland of the past."

Reactions to Brooks's piece were forceful—negative and positive alike. Many white students were defensive, claiming that their pining for the Old South was only about celebrating heritage. One letter-writer advised the editors that if they were struggling to fill column space, they were better off leaving their pages blank. Classmates pinned nasty notes to his dorm-room door and vandalized his room, but Brooks told me he was unbothered. Partly, that was because he knew he had reached other people. Students had also written to the school paper to thank him. One woman wrote that the campus should have the good sense to move away from Confederate symbolism and let Forrest's mistakes "stay buried along with his bones." And the letter got results. Brooks made his case to the student government, who then voted to remove "Dixie" from the bandstand and Forrest from the sidelines, if not the student center or the ROTC hall. But Forrest got a hero's farewell. The caption accompanying a photograph of one of the mascot's last appearances stated that Forrest "has mounted and ridden into the sunset."

NINE

Palliatives

Even after all these years, Brooks's letter still retains its rhe-
torical force, its moral clarity. Partly that's because the questions he raised are ones Americans are still asking and struggling
to answer today. "Why is it you wave your Confederate flags?
Why is it you sing your song, 'Dixie'? Why do you pay homage to
General Nathan Bedford Forrest?" he asked. "All these things are
remnants of a very old South, and have no meaningful place in
the new South that so many people are working so hard for. You
cannot seek a newer world while clinging so passionately to the
relics of days long given to the past. One cannot move forward if
his mind constantly moves backward."

Yet here we are, fifty years later. Why haven't we been able
to move forward? Searching for answers to Brooks's questions, I
paid a visit to Sarah Calise, an archivist at MTSU's Albert Gore
Research Center. The Gore Center is on the bottom floor of Todd
Hall, the university's art building. Calise was at her desk here
when the first march on Forrest Hall passed by her window in the
summer of 2015. She dropped everything, grabbed her camera,
and joined the crowd—part documentarian, part participant in
the latest battle over Forrest. Since then, Calise has been assembling a digital archive of the Forrest Hall protests. Together, we

reconnoitered in the stacks of the university's archive and talked about her work.

When Calise started documenting protests against Forrest on campus, she, too, was asking herself questions similar to those posed by Brooks. So she tried to trace the problem back to its root. When did the school start to use symbols of Forrest and, more important, why? She pulled selections of what she'd found in that hunt through the past. There were photo albums full of fraternity boys dressed up as Confederate soldiers—one from a toga-Confederate crossover party. A yearbook from the 1950s she'd pulled includes a cartoon Confederate soldier who had somehow become unstuck in time to roam the campus and to guide the reader through the book. Imagine the Microsoft paper-clip animation, but with kepi and hardtack. It's high-concept, low-production-value Confederate kitsch (a standout in that crowded subgenre). In the margin of the student organization page, the Confederate soldier, grinning ear to ear, takes from his haversack a Klan hood, as if to say: Here's our organization.

Then Calise handed me a copy of an even older yearbook, this one from 1930. A series of paintings intersperse the volume, illustrating a day in the life of a rural Tennessean: daybreak with mule and plow, an afternoon harvesting hay, a Klan lynching that evening, and dancing by the river at night. Their order restored and spirits buoyed, they can finally admit that "the sun shines as brightly and the moon as softly as it did before the war."

It is a galling and revealing glimpse of the school's collective frame of mind. The school "clung tenaciously to the Lost Cause identity prominent in the period," Derek Frisby, the chair of the task force, wrote in his essay on the school's history with Forrest, arguing that the "connection between the traditions of the Old South and the school may have served as a palliative for a campus suffering under severe economic distress." But given the nature of the imagery, this palliative was clearly prescribed for racial anxieties as much as, if not more than, economic ones.

In his assessment, Frisby echoes Andrew Lytle's appraisal of Nathan Bedford Forrest in his 1931 biography, *Bedford Forrest and His Critter Company*, in which he deemed Forrest the "spiritual comforter" of the South. The biography champions Forrest as a shining exponent of everything admirable about the yeoman South. Lytle was born in Murfreesboro into a prominent middle Tennessee family and was a descendant of Captain William Lytle, the revolutionary commander who named the town. Considered a lion of Southern letters, Andrew Lytle was part of the Southern Renaissance and the editor of *The Sewanee Review* in the 1960s. When Lytle died in 1995, an obituary in the *Review* stated that, with his death, "the Confederacy at last came to its end." If only. He's best known, though, as one of the "Agrarians" who contributed an essay to *I'll Take My Stand: The South and the Agrarian Tradition*, a collection that put forward a vision for and defense of Jeffersonian ideals rooted in the rural, the agricultural, and as the title suggests, the Old South ethos. The collection was published in 1930, the same year as the yearbook open in front of me. Industrialism had come late to the South, but when it did, the Agrarians—this collection of poets and writers and historians based at nearby Vanderbilt University—felt they'd reached the Rubicon. "Commerce cannot be assimilated to the life-pattern of the community," these twelve Southerners wrote in the cosigned introduction. Although the primary tension, in their view, was agrarian versus industrial, there were racial over-tones as well. The utopia they meant to define and defend, like that dream of the South from whence they came, conceived of a paradise only for white people. As Paul V. Murphy writes in his study of the Agrarians, *The Rebuke of History,* "At the heart of Agrarianism was the question of not only where do I stand, but also, who belongs?"

The Civil War was still so close at hand for this generation—literally, in Andrew Lytle's case. Lytle's grandmother was shot in the throat by a Union soldier in 1863. She pinned a velvet ribbon above her collar to cover the scar. Lytle kept that ribbon on his bedpost at his home in nearby Monteagle. Many of the Agrarians chose Civil War men as subjects for biographies: Allen Tate wrote one of Jefferson Davis, Robert Penn Warren (perhaps foreshadowing his ideological split with the Agrarians on issues of race) on John Brown. But for Lytle, Forrest was the paragon of the Agrarian ethos: a natural man, a frontier genius, and, as the Grand Wizard of the Klan, "The last ruler of the South."

Lytle's contribution to *I'll Take My Stand,* an essay titled "The Hind Tit," sketches a Southern idyll. He sees the Southern white yeoman as existentially untroubled, at peace with self, land, and God. "The great drain" was his term for industry. His essay features koanlike bits of argument: "A farm is not a place where you grow wealthy; it is a place where you grow corn," and "Industrialism is trying to convince the yeoman that time not space has value." But if you are going to define and defend a certain culture, you must, at some point, draw a border. Lytle notes how emancipation knocked the poor white man's sense of self akimbo: "With an entirely different race to serve the rich men as in slavery, the small white man could feel no very strong social inequality, and those who lived in isolation, none at all." But in an industrializing world came a new social hierarchy, based "not upon comparative use and enjoyment of nature, but upon a possession of cash." Lytle saw both the white Southerner's culture and self-esteem as under threat. The social stratifications wrought by industrial capitalism should be resisted, Lytle argued. Not through cross-racial class solidarity, but rather by something more recalcitrant. He ends his essay with, "It is our own, and if we have to spit in the water-bucket to keep it our own, we had better do it."

Soon after the school published their yearbook with an illustration of a lynching and Lytle published this essay, the state of Tennessee would pass laws that classified miscegenation a felony and a "one drop law" that will define any person with any African ancestry as legally Black. The year after that, men in nearby Manchester, Tennessee, lynched Richard Wilkerson, a farmhand, for allegedly slapping a white man in defense of a Black woman. It was one of over two hundred lynchings in Tennessee between 1877 and 1950. Jim Crow laws and lynchings defined and enforced the racial caste system while letting the white man know that, no matter his class, he stood above Black people. The bucket may have had spit in it, but at least it was yours.

A PALLIATIVE RELIEVES pain without curing the illness. You might think of Lytle and MTSU's pining for Forrest as symptoms of a very old, very American, madness about race. The received wisdom about race in America is that it has always been this way—racial hierarchy the original sin attending the birth of the nation. But, in fact, it was necessary to invent it. In the seventeenth century, indentured servants and prisoners of European descent provided much of the labor in Colonial Virginia. The price of the ticket across the Atlantic was paid in years of labor in the tobacco fields of the harsh, burgeoning colony. Conditions were dreadful; few survived their indenture. But as settlement continued and the colony became more established, life spans increased. It became cost-effective for planters to import a greater number of enslaved-for-life African laborers, and thus the colony's labor force became more racially mixed. Then came Bacon's Rebellion—a 1676 uprising against Governor William Berkeley by servants, enslaved Africans, and poor freedmen, all led by the colonist Nathaniel Bacon. The rebellion was not fueled by cross-racial solidarity, but instead by anger at raids by Native American tribes, which the governor was reluctant to retaliate against. Still, the rebellion did point to a problem for the colonial planter class. In a colony organized along class lines, it would be hard for the few patricians to control the many laborers. Historian Edmund S. Morgan writes in *American Slavery, American Freedom* that "It was not uncommon, for example, for servants and slaves to run away together, steal hogs together, get drunk together . . . In Bacon's Rebellion one of the last groups to surrender was a mixed band of 80 negroes and 20 servants." And so the colonial powers countered with initiatives to reorganize their new world colony along racial lines. The Virginia House of Burgesses (the legislative body of the British colony) began to legislate whiteness. The invention of race afforded a new sense of status to the pale-skinned Europeans—a palliative that could sustain the delusion.

One can see, in the years after the rebellion, the colonial powers begin to consciously construct a racial caste system, establishing Machiavellian laws that forbade free Black people and Native Americans from owning Christian servants, laws that protected the property of white servants and confiscated the property of enslaved Africans, laws that criminalized the striking of any Christian by an African or Native American, which, as Morgan writes, "allowed servants to bully slaves without fear of retaliation, thus placing them psychologically on par with masters." It is from the House of Burgesses that we see the first usage of *whiteness* (as opposed to the terms *English, European,* and *Christian*) in print in America. Then, in 1691, legislature threatened to banish any white citizens who marry someone of another race. Black translated to slave; white, no matter the class, to free. Taken together, these laws enshrined a sickness, the lie of racial difference, and with it a palliative, a psychological sense of superiority.

Race is a construct but, nevertheless, it has shaped so much of American life. As the new country grew, race became the center pole on which the country was built. The signs are evident throughout our history: the three-fifths clause in the Constitution ascribed only partial humanity to those enslaved Africans, defining their inferiority and thus justifying the cruelties of the institution; the 1790 Naturalization Act limited citizenship to "free whites of good character"; the Supreme Court's 1857 Dred Scott decision that African Americans, free or slave, had no standing to sue in federal court, as they were not citizens; into the twentieth century, the Jim Crow laws that codified public space to reflect the racial hierarchy; redlining that did the same to homes and mortgages; and the war on drugs that ensured the country's prisons did, too.

As THAT MTSU yearbook put it, happiness is having your own Confederate flag to wave at the pep rally; likewise, America's conception of race has been the kneecapping of people of color in order for white people to feel tall. But claiming an identity based on a lie deranges you. So does winning a rigged game. Just look at how white people have reacted when confronted about the lie of their racial superiority in moments such as Reconstruction and the civil rights movement: lynchings, night-riding. Terrorism. Sociopathy. Instead of admitting the lie and working to establish a true democracy, white Americans consoled themselves with palliatives—Confederate flags during the civil rights movement, the Confederate monuments during Jim Crow—and made whiteness fungible, choosing to count the Irish and the Italians, say, as white while coining markers such as "quadroon" and "octoroon" and "one-drop" to legislate Blackness. Doing so eternally emphasizes some sort of not-Blackness at the core of American whiteness. Whiteness is a void, an emptiness, a lie on which Americans birthed and built a nation.

When Sarah Calise first handed me that 1930 yearbook with the image of the Klan lynching, she noted that, "The yearbook is what you want other people to think of when they think of your school." So what is this one, with its lynching and the subsequent dancing under the moon, saying to us? How might it answer the questions raised in Sylvester Brooks's letter? That the minds of white folks still moved backward, still honored Forrest, because they still treated the same old sickness with the same salve.

When I spoke with Sylvester Brooks, he reflected on the persistence of the debate over Forrest at MTSU and connected it to the long and pernicious legacy of whiteness in the country.

"Faces have changed, uniforms have changed, but the same arguments are there," Brooks said. As a slave trader and planter, Brooks pointed out, Forrest had become one of the wealthiest men in the state of Tennessee before the war, who then joined his fellow rich white men in an effort to "convince poor whites that they were going to fight and die for a cause that was going to keep them poor and keep Blacks enslaved." And so, it seems, for as long as we organize our society along racial lines, we will continue to wrestle with these questions of prerogative and inequity. Or, in the words of Selma's former mayor James Perkins, Jr., we will continue to fight the same war with the same general.

TEN

A Letter to the Editor

March 24, 2016, the third and final forum in the battle over Forrest Hall: again the tense atmosphere, again the same debate, and again, a walkout. This time Crutchfield and Woodruff headed for the president's house, which they found cordoned off by police tape. They stood outside in the rain until Dr. McPhee agreed to meet with them. But even as they seemed to be making headway on the protest, Crutchfield was losing patience. On April 8, just a week before the task force would make their final deliberations, Crutchfield published an op-ed in the local *Daily News Journal* urging all Black students at MTSU to transfer to historically Black schools.

"From our perspective, it makes little sense that we are still engaged in a fight that should have been over decades ago," he wrote, noting that, "As a historian, this battle is less about history and more about the right of a few to desperately hold on to a legacy and heritage that valorizes a time when my ancestors were deemed less than human." Crutchfield summed up the feelings of frustration, anger, and futility he had felt over the course of a year spent having to argue that the university, to whom he paid tuition, needed to acknowledge his basic humanity. "How much longer do we have to tell you that having symbols of white supremacy on our campus doesn't exactly give us warm and fuzzy feelings?" He ended the letter by saying: "We don't have to beg institutions to be included. And we don't have to be where we're not wanted."

Crutchfield's letter echoed the letter Brooks had written half a century earlier—same fight, same general. But where Brooks's letter still saw the possibility that the school could find a new way to be, Crutchfield was bearish. Which makes sense. In Brooks's moment, in the first years after the crescendo of the civil rights movement, white Americans had an opportunity to face the malignancies on which they had built their society, and to let go of the palliatives. But while some laws had changed, hearts and minds hadn't, and inequities persisted. So Crutchfield was done explaining, done asking, done with MTSU.

Still, his letter struck a nerve.

In the task force's final deliberation—videotaped and included in Calise's archive—they were forced to take up Crutchfield's letter and discuss its ramifications. Then the forum, with several strong dissenting views, voted to recommend to the president that they change the name on the ROTC building. And, in a move that surprised many who had grown cynical over the drawn-out, fraught process, the president soon recommended the same to the Tennessee Board of Regents. That summer, the Board of Regents concurred, too. By September 2016, the university had filed an application for a waiver from the Tennessee Historical Commission to officially change the name of Forrest Hall. The commission announced that it would consider the appeal at an upcoming meeting.

A few weeks after the commission agreed to hear MTSU's

case, I asked Crutchfield if he was surprised by the initial success of the protest.

"Not at one point did I believe this is going to happen. I didn't even think it was going to get this far," he said. Surprised, yes, but hopeful? No. "I don't trust symbolic change because symbols don't change the system." But he acknowledged the importance of the symbolic work. "How can we begin to dismantle white supremacy when we can't even take down its symbols?"

I asked if, after the University's willingness to change the name, he stood by his letter encouraging students to transfer. He did. "If it's this hard to take down a symbol from the past for a war that's lost, if it's that hard, we got work to do."

ELEVEN

The Way of Forrest

During one reporting trip to Murfreesboro, I availed myself of some off-campus Civil War attractions. I headed first for Woodbury, due east of Murfreesboro on the McMinnville Highway. "Forrest Rested Here, July 12th, 1862" announces a marker posted just off the shoulder of the road. "Here Forrest, with his newly organized brigade of about 1400 cavalrymen, halted for a short rest before making his successful raid on Federal forces at Murfreesboro under Gen. T. L. Crittenden," reads the inscription. To stand where Forrest stood. Or rather, in this case, nap where Forrest napped. A little patch of hallowed ground where the shoulder's gravel bleeds out into the sloping, sunbaked grass. A creek up ahead babbled. The marker is just past a school, and since I was there during the morning hours when the enforced speed limit drops twenty miles per hour, every car that passed was either slowing to enter into the school zone or hitting the gas as they came out—it was as if I were standing in some kind of magnetic field.

All told, it was pleasant enough to linger on the shoulder of a state road. But, I admit, I was at a bit of a loss for what to do with myself. The play-by-play recitations of battles have never held my interest—I could never find the romance in it. I've always been more Gettysburg Address than Pickett's Charge, trying to understand the war in terms of its causes and consequences rather than its charges and retreats. When I spoke with Elizabeth Coker, the Old South tour guide, she suggested that this might be due to the fact I don't come from a military family. Maybe. But I can't help but be preoccupied with the stakes, what hung in the balance, what those 620,000 people died for: the unfinished work, as Lincoln put it, to ensure "that this nation, under God, shall have a new birth of freedom."

Where I was that morning wasn't a battlefield, though. It was something closer to a pilgrimage site, a stop along the Way of General Forrest. I was struck by the precision of the memory. Forrest rested exactly *here*. I began to imagine the other routine tasks his admirers might enshrine. Forrest supped here. Forrest sneezed here. Forrest asked for directions here. That last one, of course, actually exists: remember Emma Samson, the teenager in Alabama who showed Forrest a low spot in the river where he might cross and whose likeness was, in return, cast in stone at the end of Gadsden's Broad Street.

Hagiography inspires minutiae, I suppose.

From his temporary resting place, I retraced Forrest's steps down into Murfreesboro—dawn when Forrest hoofed it, midday as I drove it 154 years later. The descent from Short Mountain into the Central Basin affords some peak Tennessee views: rocky tops beyond rocky tops. It's said that, on a clear day, you can see Nashville from here, but today it's mountain silhouettes one after another, receding to a fog-fuzzed horizon. Then came rolling pastures with grazing cows and several plywood signs, TRUMP emblazoned in blue spray paint.

Reporting out these monument battles in four different cities gave me plenty of windshield time. To help pass it, I'd developed a Punch Buggy kind of game, like the one my brother and I had played as children over long drives in the back of the station wagon. Except instead of counting Volkswagens, it was bootleg Trump merch, and I didn't have anyone to sock on the arm when I saw something. Instead, I'd just wring my hands and sigh.

By October of 2016, the vivid red of the high-crowned MAGA hats and the deep blue of the Trump-Pence flags were fixtures on heads and houses wherever I went. I was more intrigued by the homemade and bootleg campaign gear—things like this plywood sign—which seemed to signal a deeper, more personal stake in the campaign. I'd been sensitized to off-brand paraphernalia like this after seeing stockpiles of it at a NASCAR race back in May.

It would be a stretch to call myself a NASCAR fan, in that I'd never actually watched (or had much of an interest in watching) a race. But a few months earlier my friend Mitch had gotten in touch, told me he wanted to come down to Alabama for the race at Talladega, and I figured what the heck. Mitch is one of my oldest and closest friends. I still have his seventh-grade school photo tucked in the cigar box on my bookshelf; he still wears the same buzz cut and the same goofy grin. If a NASCAR race was the thing to bring us together for more than a night squeezed in between family obligations at Christmas, so be it.

Stock car racing has always been an inescapable if ambient presence in my life. It was ascendant in the nineties, went mainstream as I came of age. I knew NASCAR the way a retail worker learns the words to all the Top 40 hits after a few shifts with the radio pumped in through the drop-ceiling speakers. So during that weekend with Mitch, much felt familiar, like home. The rac- ers' names and numbers came back to me like the lyrics to an old song. We pitched camp in a meadow across the street from the track, where the scene was a cross between a football tailgate, a carnival midway, and something wholly its own. There were makeshift casino tents, karaoke stages, tiki bars. In the air were the smells of cigarettes, weed, and porta-potty cleaning agents. In the waning light the atmosphere took on a hazy, uncanny feel, the edges softened by cans of suds. I admit the novelty of the scene was fun. It was like an amusement park for white guys. We lost all the cash in our pockets at a carnival game whose rules or purpose I never fully comprehended, washed down sau- sages with the beer we'd been handed by friendly passersby, and drifted through stalls of merchandise.

There was all the requisite racer gear—the colorful faux-leather jackets, those mammoth 64-oz. gas-station thermoses emblazoned with racers past and present, key rings, belt buckles, T-shirts, tank tops, flip-flops, ball caps, beanies. And mixed in with all of the racing gear was Trump gear. Heaps of it. The sheer tonnage of Trump stuff for sale was staggering, if perhaps unsurprising. And there was a whole taxonomy of apparel: Gearheads for Trump, Truckers for Trump, Bikers for Trump. Then all the "Killary" gear, too, shirts testifying to all the sexual and violent and sexually vio- lent things the wearer believes should be done to the Democratic nominee—a bracing reminder that the night wouldn't have felt like an amusement park for people who didn't look like me and Mitch.

This was late May 2016, almost a year since Donald Trump rode down his gold-colored escalator to announce his candi- dacy in a speech in which he referred to Mexicans as rapists. A few months later, he called for a total ban on Muslim immigration to the United States. These displays of nativism, combined with vague assurances of prosperity for the long-suffering white working class, continued through the early primaries. Trump finished second in January's Iowa Caucuses, then took the New Hampshire primary. Reports of violence at his rallies that spring only served to make his campaign a media spectacle, amplifying his demagoguery and consolidating his support. Just a few weeks before the Talladega race, he'd torched Ted Cruz in Indiana to become the Republican Party's presumptive nominee.

The morning of the race, I emerged from our tent bleary-eyed, smelling like soot and curdled milk. I headed for a porta-potty for my a.m. ablutions. By force of habit, I perused the graffiti on the walls. Mostly it was the usual reststop "For a good time, call ... " scribblings. But next to the empty hand-sanitizer dispenser was this: "If I was a damn dirty Mexican I'd go ahead and shoot myself."

That afternoon, hungover in the stands, I kept one eye on the race and the other on gathering storm clouds, but saw mostly that line scrawled onto the blue plastic siding. I was appalled by the sentiment but fascinated by the phrasing, the twisted self-loathing of it. It wasn't saying Mexicans—the others—should die. It was saying that, if *I* were a Mexican, I would hate myself enough to kill myself. Apparently, the only thing keeping the writer of that sentiment from suicide was their whiteness. That old bucket still held water, it seems, and a great deal more spit.

Brad Keselowski took the checkered flag that afternoon, but I couldn't tell you how. Mitch and I walked out of the speedway in a sea of people retreating to their cars and campers, nearly all of them white and many sporting Trump gear they'd picked up on the midway. I considered for the first time that Trump could actually win the presidency, and saw how he might do it.

BACK IN MURFREESBORO, I descended into the valley and passed the fortifications of strip malls that surrounded the city. I turned onto East Main and puttered through a quaint residential neighborhood before arriving on the square. Murfreesboro is the geographic center of Tennessee. At the center of the town square sits the courthouse—a three-story brick building, columned, corniced, and clock-towered. A small plaque on a bench facing the courthouse doors read "Rutherford County Chamber of Commerce encourages you to discover the heart of Tennessee." So there I was: at the middle of Middle Tennessee, the heart of the heart. There's a Confederate Memorial statue on the northeast corner of the square: a soldier mid-stride, with musket and haversack, facing north. *NEVER RETREAT.* Confederate symbolism is a bit laughable in its predictability, even as its glum sentimentality and its racism are anything but. As such, only the heroics of the Lost Cause are mentioned on the square. Plaques about Forrest and the Confederacy dot the courthouse. "The beginning of a legend," one is subtitled.

Having caught his winks in Woodbury, Forrest came into the city with the sunrise; dramatic lighting for the beginning of this legend. It was the morning of his forty-first birthday. And it was a homecoming, too, as he was born only twenty-five miles from there. Horses' hooves woke John Anderson from his sleep in the city jail, where he was being held by Union officers for insubordination, set for execution that day. "I shall never forget the appearance of General Forrest on that occasion; his eyes were flashing as if on fire, his face was deeply flushed, and he seemed in a condition of great excitement," Anderson remembered. The Union soldier guarding the men in the jail set fire to the floor when he heard Forrest approach. "To our horror we realized he was determined to burn us to death before the rescue party could break open the door," writes Anderson.

After rescuing the prisoners, Forrest headed across the street to storm the courthouse and smoke out the sharpshooters, then shrewdly negotiated the surrender of the rest of the Union troops. All in all, about as successful as a raid could be. "[Forrest] became overnight their particular idea of what a soldier should be," Andrew Lytle writes, claiming that after the raid, women in Middle Tennessee would threaten to set Forrest on occupying Union soldiers. "He was a bogeyman they all believed in." Lytle concludes his account of the raid with a story about a woman who approached Forrest as he made to leave town, requesting that he rear back on his horse so that she might scoop into her kerchief a bit of dirt from under the steed's hoof. Forrest obliged.

IT TOOK SOME asking down at the Heritage Center, a few blocks off the square, but finally someone in a back room was able to dig up an old photograph of the courthouse square and pointed out, in a shadowy corner, a canvas awning. The former slave market, now unmarked, occupies the corner of Church and College—just a block off the square and on a direct sightline with the courthouse statue of the Confederate soldier. It's a long stone building, two-story, painted a neutral grayish green. "Built 1843 / Repaired 1873" reads the date stone.

This tableau at the heart of the heart of Tennessee neatly arranges the contradiction at the heart of Confederate memory: Honor the soldier but make no mention (at least in public) of the actual cause for which he fought. Derek Alderman, the University of Tennessee expert on monuments and memorials, pointed out to me that even though Confederate monuments are ostensibly about remembering the past, "[they] can also be about facilitating forgetting . . . the public is encouraged to see the past in one way. So inherently it is being encouraged not to remember another part of the past."

In their documents of secession, Mississippi avowed, "Our position is thoroughly identified with the institution of slavery—the greatest material interest of the world." Two months later, Confederate vice-president Alexander H. Stephens would announce that the Confederacy's cornerstone rested upon "the great truth that the negro is not equal to the white man; that slavery, subordination to the superior race, is his natural and normal condition." They were waging the war to maintain their states' rights to hold slaves, to expand their slave society further west into the frontier, and they were making no secret about it. And yet, though slavery was their "greatest material interest" and white supremacy their foundational belief, the slave market now goes unmarked.

When I spoke with Steve Murphree, who testified before the task force in support of keeping Forrest Hall and who is the chaplain of the Murfreesboro Sons of Confederate Veterans, he told me that each year the troop marks Forrest's birthday by supping on sweet potatoes and black-eyed peas, reenacting Forrest's celebratory meal the night of the Murfreesboro raid. "Some people say we're overly romantic," Murphree said. "And we just might be guilty of that, but we're just trying to protect the good name of the Confederate soldier."

But protecting the good name of Confederate soldiers requires forgetting. And so the campaign to extract slavery from the Confederacy becomes a necessary fiction. It lays down cover—lets you continue to revere, in public, an armed campaign to create an ethnostate in thirteen former American states. Jefferson Davis, the president of the Confederacy, understood this well. In 1860, Davis proclaimed that, "We recognize the fact of the inferiority stamped upon that race of men by the Creator, and from the cradle to the grave, our Government, as a civil institution, marks that inferiority." Before long, Davis would revise his own history; in his post-war memoirs he claims slavery to be "not the cause, but an incident."

And so through remembering by forgetting—the method blueprinted in downtown Murfreesboro—we arrive at the preposterous and yet all-too-common refrain of "heritage not hate." Thus, those advocating for MTSU to keep Forrest's name could, with a straight face, claim a martial heritage without mentioning that it derives from a war waged on the belief that many of the students in the room were, because of their race, inferior.

This is what ideology does. We don't adapt our views based on the facts at hand, we assemble facts based on our ideology. We remember what we like. And white Americans are well practiced in this magical thinking, this selective memory. American exceptionalism dictates that we are entitled to a good history as our birthright—received wisdom that, in the defense of our good name, encourages white Americans to be less than critical about our past. The aspirations of our founding documents are, indeed, commendable. But, in order to maintain moral authority, our collective memory holds that we have already achieved them. As many a flag-pin-wearing politician will tell you, that's what makes us the greatest nation in the history of the world. And so we overlook how the American flag flew over a slave society for more than eighty years. Likewise we ask not what the three-fifths clause in that sacrosanct Constitution says about who we are, morally. We leave unanswered the question of to whom, exactly, the "we" in "We the people" refers. Or, for that matter, that the US only became a true democracy with the passage of the Voting Rights Act in 1965. "Slavery looms up mountainously," wrote Robert Penn Warren of the legacy of the Civil War, but we're more likely to look away to the roadside where Forrest slept, more likely to paint over the slave market. This keeps intact the things we want to believe about our country, our past, our present, ourselves.

On the day of my visit to downtown Murfreesboro, early voting was underway in Tennessee for the 2016 presidential election—an election that was proving to be another referendum on our memory, and our forgetting, of American history. At the polling place on the outer ring of the courthouse square, a line of people snaked out the door and halfway down the block. Many were there, no doubt, to cast votes for Donald Trump, whose campaign slogan, "Make America Great Again," could only be admired via the remembering and forgetting at work here on the courthouse square, and whose signature policy proposal was to build a two-thousand-mile monument along the southern border. He'd win Tennessee handily. When Pennsylvania was called in his favor, too, his path to victory was clear.

TWELVE

More Gump than Bedford

During that October visit to Middle Tennessee, Forrest's name still stood above the doors of the ROTC building, though by then it was in bureaucratic purgatory. The Historical Commission had agreed to hear the University's request but had yet to set a date for deliberation. From the courthouse square, I headed back to campus thinking that it might be the last time I'd see it while the ROTC building was still named for Forrest. Middle Tennessee State's campus is long, flat, and low—the buildings like haystacks in a meadow. I came up on Forrest Hall slowly, hobbling with a bum ankle I'd recently injured while playing pickup soccer. Compared to the admissions building where I got my parking pass and the student union across from it—all glass and curving lines—Forrest Hall's brick and mortar felt like an anachronism, there on the eastern end of campus. Inside it felt even older: with the yellow fluorescent light and mildew smell of a dilapidated gymnasium covered by what I described in my notes as a "Lysol factory meltdown." Despite my ankle, I did a lap, inspected the medals in the trophy case and the photographs of enlisted students framed and on the wall, poked my head into empty, standard-looking classrooms. I'm not sure what I expected, but there wasn't much to see. No stray Confederate-flag sticker on the lockers in the bathroom, no Sons of Confederate Veterans flyers in the rack of recruitment brochures, no likeness of Forrest in the portraits of old commanders.

After poking around for a while, I went back outside and sat on a bench. Just down from me was a bus-stop overhang, and I watched students gather and board, gather and board. Out here I could feel it—the thing I'd been searching for inside, some disturbance in the energy of the place. A friend once told me that if you don't believe in ghosts, you won't see ghosts. At this point, it's safe to say I not only believed in Forrest's ghost but was actively calibrating my Confederate spectrometer. Others have felt it, too, though for different reasons. Students of color testified at the forums that they avoided the building because they do not want to think about the man who did not think them human. I stretched my ankle and watched a few more buses go by as I thought about how there are no bus stops I've ever waited at, could ever wait at, really, that I would go out of my way to avoid. None that could remind me that others considered me sub-human. Instead, I waited at bus stops named for men who built this country with me in mind.

I experienced a bracing reminder of this influence when digging through the school's archive. Perusing the pages of a fraternity scrapbook Calise pulled for me, full of snapshots, one after another, of all the frat brothers dressed in gray, of all the mascots parading down East Main St. in boots and duster, it struck me that I look a lot like Forrest: six foot two, 180 pounds, scraggly beard, unkempt hair, and with his cold blue eyes, and so I might have celebrated a Middle Tennessee touchdown atop a horse renamed King Philip, as Sylvester Brooks looked on from the stands feeling some part derision, some part repulsion, and some other part forever unimaginable to me. When I embarked on this journey, I expected that the longer I worked at it, the more people I spoke with, the more reasons I would find to decry Forrest. And that's been true. What I didn't expect was to be forced to consider our connection, our proximity. I can reject every tenet of the Confederacy and yet the fact remains that, in fighting to maintain white supremacy, Forrest sought to perpetuate a system tilted in my favor. Forrest fought for me. The work was to understand the proximity, not the distance. Not to try to imagine bus stops and buildings that I'd avoid, but to understand why we've needed to build the ones that others were avoiding. But, of course, it's our prerogative to ignore these questions if we so please.

In an essay for *The New York Times*, Eula Biss writes that the condition of white life is one of "forgotten debt." "Not a kinship or a culture," Biss writes of the essence of whiteness, as genetics does not identify any closer relationship among white people than between white and Black people. "American definitions of race allow for a white woman to give birth to Black children, which should serve as a reminder that white people are not a family," Biss continues. Instead, white people are confederates in a lie meant to protect our advantages, dating back to the colonial era. Whiteness is a coalition of power among a loose, shifting group of pale-skinned European Americans. The courthouse statue that pretends it cannot see the slave yard.

But what debts did I owe to whiteness? When my family moved from Philadelphia to rural Lancaster County and my parents bought their first house, the likelihood of them securing

120

Down Along with That Devil's Bones

a mortgage for a home in a "good" neighborhood with a "good" school district had much to do with their whiteness. At high school parties, my ability to run from police officers into the surrounding cornfields without fear, without even a second thought to what might happen next, was surely an indulgence provided by the color of my skin. When I graduated high school and needed loans to attend a "good" college, my parents co-signed for me, having, as they did, the backing of their home mortgage. Sufficiently propped up by modest intergenerational wealth, I've now ventured forth into the crumbling field of journalism—a decision made with the tacit assumption that, should I fail, I had generations of family members who would provide for me in my hour of need with a place to crash, money for rent, and professional connections to start again in education, medicine, public relations. Sure, my parents worked hard. And yes, they are upstanding, empathic people committed to social justice who raised their four sons to be the same. That doesn't mean our lives aren't shaped and mangled by our race—a fact we have the luxury of seeing or not seeing.

But these reporting trips had made my whiteness, as the Russian writer Victor Shklovsky might put it, defamiliarized. Shklovsky's idea was that the role of art is to "make the stone stony," to disrupt all we'd been habitualized to, and thus be able to see it anew. And here, on the yard of Forrest's last toehold on campus, the stone was stony.

Brooding there on the bench, I watched another round of buses come and go, and couldn't help but think of *Forrest Gump*. Tom Hanks's titular character spends the majority of that movie at a bus stop, prattling on about his life to anyone who will listen.

Early in the film, he accounts for his name. The screen flickers sepia, and Hanks, dressed in a white bed sheet as his namesake Nathan Bedford Forrest, ambles up on horseback. His name, he says in that affected drawl, is meant "to remind me that sometimes people do stupid things," then describes how "we was related to him in some way."

In tracing a history from Bedford Forrest to Bear Bryant, polio to AIDS, Cold War conflict to ping-pong diplomacy, the Hanks movie reflects white Americans' desperate desire for a happy history, to be reassured that although we have done some stupid things, we are always, inevitably, at the center of a sweeping, noble tale, with a daffy smile and an eager wave. We should feel proud of our past, goddammit. And what's more, we should derive from that pride a divinely sanctioned sense of our own innocence. A reassuring story to tell yourself, no doubt, but a deluded one. If only we would sit at bus stops in the discomfiting silence that comes with the knowledge that we are instead antagonists, that we are implicated, if only passively, in a centuries-long campaign of oppression and extraction. A campaign waged in our name and for our pockets. Not the most pleasant way to pass the time, I admit, which is probably why we've developed such extraordinary ways to avoid doing it. But if we are ever to gain a clearer sense of who we've been, and thus who we are as white Americans, we are going to need to revise the story.

WHEN PROTESTERS BURIED Forrest in effigy last year, they left his body in a coffin on the steps. Out on the bench, I was suddenly seized by an urge to find it. I got up and went back into Forrest Hall. I poked my head into every office, asking if anyone knew about that protest last year? About the name of this building? I think they left a papier-mâché doll on the steps? Any chance you know what happened to it? Eyebrows raised, then furrowed into frowns. Some remembered the protests, fewer the funeral, none the whereabouts of the body. One asked if it was mine.

Yes, I wanted to say. He's mine.

THIRTEEN

A Flag in War

In late February, 2018, the Tennessee Historical Commission ruled on the university's petition to change the name of Forrest Hall: waiver denied. Sarah Calise was in South Carolina when she heard the news. She was not surprised by the ruling, "but still very disappointed," she told me. Crutchfield's reaction was ambivalent and left him in search of a silver lining. "Of course you don't want to see something that you worked really, really hard on be unsuccessful, but you have to define success for yourself. Is success the ultimate goal of getting the name down? Is it starting the conversation? Is it mobilizing students who weren't motivated politically before this? If you look at the entire process, you can definitely see some successes there, but the ultimate goal didn't happen." Fighting against racial inequality is a hard, long battle, he explained, and it's often necessary to reframe a campaign to emphasize the positives. "In any type of social-justice movement for change, you have to redefine success or you will be depressed all the time."

Calise was more upset. The campaign was "one of the most frustrating things I've ever had to go through as a historian," she told me. The futility of trying to impress upon people the facts of Forrest's life, much less the consequences of those facts—it vexed her. "Him being a military strategist means more to you than the fact that for fifty years, students have been offended and scared to walk by a building—that's what I can't come to terms with. Why does your love for this dude outweigh your respect for another human being?"

I put that question to Elizabeth Coker. She attributed it to the import she places on military history. Her father fought in World War II, her grandfather in World War I, and "both of them were descendants of Confederate Veterans," she responded. She draws a straight line from that lineage to the things that are right and good in the country today. And she brooks no dissent from that point of view. Anyone who fails to see the inherent goodness in that legacy demonstrates "their ignorance of what made this country great."

Competing histories and competing grievances had made the Forrest debate an exercise in prerogative. In other words, the debate turned on collective memory more than history. And this is the rub of collective memory, it's not always so "collective." The teller of a story often needs to have a similar background to the listener for the story to land, to resonate across the web of shared experience and beliefs. "A narrative that runs counter to dominant politics or ideology will prove hard to communicate," writes Erika Apfelbaum, a scholar of collective memory. Memory is self-reinforcing, and thus self-insulating. It creates an adversarial relationship so that protests from outside a given group fall on deaf ears. Southern historian C. Vann Woodward called this gap between living memory and written history a "twilight zone," that serves as "one of the favorite breeding grounds of mythology." An intervention into Forrest's legend would have to come from within.

Dr. Frisby, the chair of the task force, had always been bearish on the possibility of the Historical Commission granting a waiver in the case. The commission is in the business of preserving history, he told me, and these new powers vested in them by the Heritage Preservation Act were outside of their purview. "This is a power they never asked for and aren't set up to handle," he said. Permitting the school to change the name would set a precedent, he predicted: "As soon as they approve a waiver, a storm's going to come." When I asked Dr. Frisby if he thought anyone had changed their mind about Forrest over the course of the debate, he just chuckled.

The task force had devoted months to the debate, hearing two mutually exclusive versions of Forrest. Then the State Board of Regents and the Tennessee Historical Commission—two different groups of prominent, powerful Tennesseans—each debated the issue and came to two opposite conclusions. At the end, it was hard not to see it as an exercise in futility, a year's worth of evidence of just how fractured American memory is.

The frustrations of this campaign prompted Joshua Crutchfield to reassess his aims in activism, getting him to focus more on systems of inequity rather than the symbols of that inequity. "I think symbols have power," he explains. "If there's ever a time that that's evident, it's now. [But] there's a system that upholds those symbols. I don't know which one comes first. Maybe you get rid of the system and the symbols come down." But protests over symbols can sometimes feel reactionary, he reflected. Someone else puts up a monument or names a building and then there you are, channeling all your energy into getting it down, allowing your opponent to set the terms of the debate.

"Where do we start to be more strategic about implementing systems within ourselves and our communities?" he asked aloud. One answer, for Crutchfield, has been to shift his attentions to organizing in Nashville, working as a part of the local Black Lives Matter chapter to create a community oversight program for policing in the city. Being proactive, organizing communities, holding systems of power to account for abuse and mistreatment: "That's the path forward at this point."

But, he added, as long as those symbols are still up, they are "like a flag in war."

PART THREE

This Is Us

Nashville

FOURTEEN

At the Foot of the
Ugliest Confederate Memorial

Head north on I-65 and you'll see it on your right, after you've coiled through Franklin, Tennessee, past the Nissan North America headquarters, past the Walmart and the Galleria, up through Brentwood's leafy burbs, just across the Nashville city limits. From peripheral vision at 70 mph, it scans as little more than a shock of silver and gold, like someone slipped a single Civil War image into a film reel of fast-food franchises, firework megastores, and the rest of the visual muddle of highway travel. Still, it's unmistakable. And if you pull onto the shoulder and get out for closer inspection, you'll see, beyond the kudzu-threaded barbed-wire fence and inside a half-circle of Confederate battle flags, the horse and rider, Lieutenant General Nathan Bedford Forrest astride his steed, twenty-seven feet from horse hoof to saber tip, riding parallel to the roadway. The statue sits on private property, hence the barbed wire. It is highly visible but only from a distance and only for a moment; a flicker of Forrest as you enter the city.

Behold: our nation's ugliest Confederate statue. It is crudely and cartoonishly rendered in plastic, Forrest in silver, his horse in gold. Forrest brandishes a pistol, an elongated arm protruding from his shoulder at a grotesque angle, his too-large head turned unnaturally to stare at traffic. His face is contorted, his eyebrows raised and his teeth bared, as if in the middle of a rebel yell. It is so absurd and tacky that it must be a joke—the sculpting crude, the likeness farcical, the colors ridiculous—but no: it was carved and erected in sincerity.

The artist responsible for this roadside travesty is Jack Kershaw, a longtime Nashville resident, who sculpted it between 1996 and 1998. Kershaw was an unreconstructed Renaissance man—a painter, sculptor, lawyer, semi-pro quarterback, grass-roots organizer, and avowed racist. When Kershaw died in 2010, an obituary submitted to the Nashville *Tennessean* called him a "gold-plated eccentric," while the Southern Poverty Law Center went with "one of the most iconic American white segregation-ists of the 20th century," noting his role in founding multiple white-supremacist organizations along with his bizarre contri-bution to the country's collection of Confederate monuments.

For years, I've been both fascinated and repulsed by the statue, gnarled and nightmarish, and the life of its creator. The story of the statue and artist points both forward and backward in time—tracing a line from the Agrarians of the Jim Crow era up to the roiling heart of American madness at present. And so, wanting a better look at the statue of Forrest than the glimpse afforded by the interstate, I got ahold of William Dorris, who owns the land upon which the statue stands, and arranged a visit.

Under a light rain on a winter Monday in 2017, I turned onto Regent Drive, dipped under a railroad bridge, and swung past an entrance gate secured with six padlocks and several No Trespassing signs. I parked, climbed a gravel path lined with old bath fixtures, and met Dorris at the foot of the statue. Dorris is in his eighties and, as he described himself, "90 percent blind." He wore a black-and-white-checked shirt and bolo tie under his teal jacket, with thick-framed eyeglasses under wraparound black sunglasses. He leaned on a walking stick as we inspected the statue.

Dorris is retired now, but as the longtime owner of a bathroom outfitter called Aqua Bath, he provided Kershaw, a lifelong friend, with the space to sculpt on-site and the materials necessary to remember Forrest to interstate travelers. He estimated he'd spent about $80,000 on the statue since work began in the mid-nineties.

Up close, it is even more gruesome than it appears from the interstate. The effect approaches what I'd imagine it's like to be the human in a live-action animated film—like a Space Jam of the Confederacy. The statue is constructed from polystyrene blocks, and you can see both the crude execution—"he carved it with a butcher's knife," Dorris told me—and the lingering evidence of the many attempts to deface it. Anticipating that it would be a target for vandalism, Kershaw finished the statue with an anti-graffiti polish. Dorris appreciates Kershaw's prescience, as trespassers come regularly. There's a rail line abutting the statue—the Nashville & Decatur. Forrest raided it multiple times during the war, Dorris told me. More recently, someone tried to topple the statue by tying one end of the cable to the horse, the other to a train in the rail yard below. After that, Dorris added a support beam to the horse's hind legs. So far, it's held on. It has likewise survived several shootings and numerous calls for the city to build a wall or plant shrubbery to block the view from the highway. When one such protest came in the summer of 2015, Dorris suggested that he could put the statue on stilts to display it above any barrier the city might build.

Standing there at the foot of the statue, I started to pick up on a strange kind of honesty in it—the fever-dream impressionism somehow offers, to my mind, a more accurate view of Confederate history than, say, Forrest's stately equestrian statue in Memphis or the bust, inconspicuous and modest, further north in the Tennessee Capitol. Forrest should look this ugly, this preposterous, in our remembrances. "Let that one stay up," more than one activist has told me, as if the statue were the portrait of a Confederate Dorian Gray.

We stayed at the statue's foot for about fifteen minutes, staring up at it, long enough for me to get, and then get used to, a crick in my neck. Then Dorris took me on a lap of the narrow grounds on which the statue sits. Dorris moved delicately with his cane on the gravel but did so with an intuitive, almost uncanny sense of the grounds. As we started down the hill away from the statue, he pulled up suddenly and said, "We're probably just at the corner of the old ice house."

You couldn't draw a straighter line from his toes to where the stones met at the corner of a mostly collapsed building, about ten feet from the gravel path. There's an artesian well nearby and, before the war, enslaved people laid the stones for an ice house. What remained was mostly foundation, set below the surface of the sloping land. Most ruins bring to mind what once was there, prompting you to mentally project an overlay of a completed structure, like a visual autocorrect. But not with this. What struck me about it was what was there, still—a carved-out bit of land, forever blocked in stone, the land reshaped, the stones unyielding. The labor of the enslaved people who built this country remained as a kind of negative space. It was the inverse of the statue on the other side of the workshed. Like the forgotten corner near the courthouse square in Murfreesboro that once held the slave market, here is another memorial that holds a story that a monument won't tell.

After inspecting the icehouse, I rejoined Dorris and we continued our walk. He had just started to explain something about Forrest and the train line when he stopped short again. We were at the far corner of the icehouse now. It was like out of the movies, what he was doing. He must be messing with me, I thought. Some obtuse joke on the interloping journalist. Maybe he wasn't as blind as he had let on? I doubted it. More likely, he just knows the land so well, has walked the knowledge of it into his nerve endings. If I lay down, he said, right at the corner of the building and used its edge as a sight line, I should be able to see the farmhouse of the family who lived on this land before the war. I obliged, crouching and aligning, but mostly I just saw the interstate. I got up a few times to reposition, searching for some crack in the Impalas and retaining walls to see what Dorris wanted me to see. But I couldn't. Whatever Dorris was seeing behind those two pairs of glasses, for the life of me, I couldn't see it.

After the battles of Franklin and Nashville in December of 1864, this land was a field hospital, Dorris told me. What is now his workshed was then a stable, repurposed to care for wounded soldiers. Over one thousand Confederate soldiers died in the Battle of Franklin just down the road, fifteen hundred more in the battle of Nashville, fought just north of where we were. "I could have trodden on a dead man at every step," a military chaplain said as he walked the field the morning after the Battle of Franklin. Field nurses laid out officers on the porch of a nearby house—perhaps the one Dorris was trying to get me to see. The losses here in late 1864 had doomed the Confederate effort in the western theater. Forrest would soldier on for another year, but it was, by then, futile.

After a while, I stopped pretending to be able to see the house or whatever it was I was supposed to see beyond the interstate, got up, and walked back to the statue. Dorris invited me into the workshop, and so we slouched for a while in recliners, sipping bottles of water. He sat facing the door, a box of shotgun shells to one side, to the other a bookcase with titles like *The Jewish Confederates*, *Myths and Realities of American Slavery*, and binders of Aqua Bath annual reports. Before I could even ask a question, Dorris launched into a defense of Forrest's record, telling me that even Sherman defended Forrest in his memoir.

I was more interested in hearing about Kershaw, the artist, but Dorris continued on for some time, reciting defense after defense of Forrest's record. It was like watching someone practice karate alone, parrying invisible challenges.

On the question of Forrest's slave-trading: The Cherokees did it, too. On the broader question of Forrest's views on white supremacy: If he was racist, then how did he go to sleep during the war protected by seven Black "bodyguards"? On the frequent accusations that the statue is racist: We had a Black man speak at the unveiling.

The conversation was sometimes as difficult to follow as it was to listen to, though it did suggest that our current strain of

political rhetoric—fact-allergic and driven by false equivalency—
had its roots in the Lost Cause apologia. The whataboutism, the
plausible deniability, the dog-whistles that dip, not infrequently,
into the audible range. Donald Trump would be inaugurated as
president in less than a week; it all felt so familiar.

About an hour into my visit, Dorris and I were joined by
a tall, jovial man who introduced himself as Ross. He gave off
a fraternal, *isn't this fun!?* vibe while we toured the rest of the
workshop. As we inspected Dorris's impressive collection of old
tractors, Ross told me that he had more fun with Kershaw than
anyone his own age, even as Kershaw got on into his nineties.
The two would drink scotch before a roaring fire in the hearth
of Kershaw's house. To his friends, Kershaw was charismatic, I
came to understand—eccentric and endearing. To further under-
score this point, Dorris told me the two had met when Kershaw
was driving through Dorris's neighborhood in a convertible
Studebaker, a goat in the backseat.

JACK KERSHAW WAS born in 1913, grew up in Old
Hickory, Tennessee, and attended a military school at Stone
Mountain, Georgia, where the mountainside Confederate bas-
relief sculpture looms and where William J. Simmons had
founded the second incarnation of the Ku Klux Klan in 1915. As
an undergraduate at Vanderbilt in the early thirties, Kershaw
studied geology, history, and art, and played on the football
team. He fell in with the Vanderbilt Agrarians, twelve of whom
had recently published their manifesto, *I'll Take My Stand*. Their
essentialist view of Southern identity resonated with Kershaw,
an idea he worked to incorporate into his art. Toward the end of

his time at Vanderbilt, Kershaw married Mary Noel, a cousin of Andrew Lytle, the Agrarian who wrote so admiringly of Forrest.

Mary Noel came from money; her father was a wealthy real-estate man in Nashville. When the Depression hit and golfers stopped coming to the Glendale Country Club, which he owned, he let the newlyweds live in it. Kershaw got into real estate with his father-in-law, joined a semi-professional football team in Nashville, and turned the locker room of his country club estate into a painting studio, where he set about developing his self-consciously Southern artistic vision.

But before Kershaw became obsessed with Forrest—or rather, before that obsession compelled him to make Forrest part of the daily commute of thousands of Nashville residents—he had a long career of upholding white supremacy in the South. The first white supremacist organization Kershaw founded was known as the Tennessee Federation for Constitutional Government. He launched it with Donald Davidson, another of the Agrarians. Both Kershaw and Davidson were card-carrying members of the States Rights Party, and together they coordinated statewide resistance to school integration in the state in the 1950s.

The Supreme Court's landmark ruling in Brown v. Board of Education found that school segregation violated the Equal Protection Clause of the Fourteenth Amendment. The historic decision did not, however, include specific instructions to remedy the school systems' problems. And the backlash was swift. Two weeks after the ruling in 1954, a Mississippi judge named Tom P. Brady delivered a speech that came to be known as the "Black Monday Speech," in which he called for the popular election of Supreme Court justices, for a forty-ninth state to be created and given to African Americans, and most urgently, for each Southern state to form a "law-abiding" resistance movement to integration. That movement took shape as White Citizens Councils, known colloquially as country club Klans for their insistence on so-called above-board ways to resist integration. Why burn a cross when you could foreclose a mortgage?, the logic went. Copies of Brady's "Black Monday" speech made their way across the South, and a year later there were 80,000 councilors in sixty-five Mississippi counties. Their motto was "states rights and racial integrity."

Kershaw's Tennessee Federation for Constitutional Government served as the state's incarnation of the White Citizens Council and the only statewide organization resisting integration. When, in 1956, the Tennessee NAACP filed suit to force the state to comply with the Supreme Court's ruling, Kershaw mounted the grassroots resistance. He led campaigns in places like Clinton, where a week's worth of agitating the local whites led to three nights of rioting, a siege of the county courthouse, and the deployment of the National Guard. The next year, during protests against the integration of Nashville's schools, a protester detonated a bundle of dynamite at the Hattie Cotton Elementary School.

Kershaw's efforts with the TFCG were calamitous but, ultimately, unsuccessful. So in the 1960s, Kershaw went back to school, earning a degree from the Nashville YMCA Night School of Law. In the mid-1970s, he landed James Earl Ray as a client. Since almost immediately after submitting his guilty plea for the murder of Dr. King in 1968, Ray had maintained his innocence—that he had been involved in a conspiracy led by a mysterious blond-haired

Latino man named Raul. By the time he hired Kershaw, Ray had cycled through a progression of lawyers, exhausting his appeals. So Kershaw, with no recourse in the courts, found a more creative way to represent his client. He ran with the Raul story. You can see him in TV news footage from 1977, after Ray had tried to escape from prison, dressed in a light suit, all collars and lapels, with a flop of white hair across his long forehead, promising to produce a picture of Raul should his client be granted a new trial. Short of that, he attempted to retry the case in the court of public opinion, arranging for his client to sit for an interview with *Playboy* magazine while taking a polygraph test. But the polygraph determined Ray was lying when he denied killing Dr. King—further weakening the credibility of his "Raul" theory. And when Ray discovered that Kershaw received $11,000 from the magazine for arranging the interview, he canned his lawyer.

After that, Kershaw retreated from the public eye, but he reemerged in the mid-nineties as the founder of yet another white supremacist organization. In 1994, Kershaw, the history professor Michael Hill, and some forty other white Southerners convened in the conference room of an Alabama Best Western for a three-day summit on what they felt was the deterioration of Southern culture. Calling themselves the Southern League (they would later change it to the League of the South, after a complaint from a baseball league with the same name), they focused on the "Cultural, social, economic, and political independence and well-being of the Southern people." Like the Agrarians before them, and the Confederates before *them*, the South they envisioned was a monolithic one, a white one. Their goal, as they put it in all sincerity, was to secede.

The League's secessionist bent is based on a dubious idea known as the "Celtic thesis"—an attempt to trace a line from the Celtic cultures of Central and Northern Europe on down to the European settlers of the seventeenth-century American South and into the present day. The idea being that "the South" constituted a distinct ethnic group and this was thus their homeland—as if to say, their blood, their soil. In the early years, the League acted as reactionary provocateurs—prototrolls, really—railing against the ascendant values of diversity and multiculturalism during the 1990s. As more and more people of color took to city council seats, city halls, state and national Congress, they presented counter-narratives to the white Southern identity in the centers of power—a second Reconstruction, brought on by the civil rights movement. As unreconstructed whites tried to cling to power and prerogative, so they clung to their myths and heroes. "Southerners who have studied American history and learned its lessons understand that the late unpleasantness is not over," Michael Hill, a cofounder of the League, wrote in an op-ed in 1997. "Rather, it has shifted from the battlefield to the mind and the heart, and the stake is western civilization itself... Multiculturalism and diversity are merely the code words for the destruction of western Christian civilization."

While Hill penned letters, Jack Kershaw asked his friend William Dorris for some bath-fixture material. He was ready to sculpt his masterpiece. For eighteen months, he worked like a man possessed, finishing the higher portions of his statue with a cherry picker. Near the end, Ross remembered, Kershaw fell from the lift, knocking himself out cold. After a short hospitalization, he immediately returned to work. The urgency Kershaw felt to finish the Forrest statue might go some way toward explaining the subpar execution. The model looked really impressive, Ross insisted. But he was on deadline, plus Kershaw had inexplicably become obsessed with painted Roman statuary. That's why, Ross told me, the finished statue looked like it could be on a mini-golf course.

(When I bumped into Ross again, later that day, at the Panera by the interstate on-ramp, he again felt compelled to account for the statue's ugliness. It was one of those uncanny "New South" moments where you could spend the morning in a workshop in the shadow of a Confederate statue then head up the road a mile for a chipotle-chicken panini in a strip mall. Ross didn't seem to mind, though. He did want to stress, however, that from the point of view of Nashville Confederates, it was like a badge of honor—previously they didn't have a Forrest statue and now they do.)

Aesthetics aside, Dorris and Ross told me about how excited they were to dedicate the statue. "I was in the paper forty-three days in a row," Dorris told me of the lead-up to the dedication, a note of pride ringing through his thin voice. "That's better than Elvis." Dorris explained that the original plan was to hold the dedication here, by the roadside—"He wanted to back traffic up to Alabama." But the July day in 1998 proved too hot for them to hold the ceremony outdoors. Instead, the group decamped for the nearby Overton High School gymnasium. Even so, someone fainted. Michael Hill gave the keynote address, telling hundreds of sweaty Forrest admirers that "there can be no peace until we are a separate and free people again. The day of apologizing for the conduct of our Confederate ancestors is over."

They clearly enjoyed the provocation. Dorris told me that he and Kershaw used to sit in lawn chairs in front of the statue and wave at passing cars. The statue proved to be Kershaw's piece de resistance. Tennessee schools had integrated despite Kershaw's best efforts. James Earl Ray had canned him after the hijinks with *Playboy*. But radical organization and their ludicrous statue proved to be the right methods at the right moment to make a lasting point. Enter Nashville from the south and you enter under the banner of Forrest—a move as devious as the statue is ugly. A few years after the dedication, the League submitted a request to Congress for $5 billion dollars in reparations. Reparations, that is, to white landowners for the destruction of their land during the Civil War. The next year, when a reporter for the New Orleans *Times-Picayune* pressed Kershaw about the Forrest statue, the artist responded: "Someone needs to say a good word for slavery."

But by the aughts, Kershaw was in his 90s; he wouldn't live to see Confederate statues and the League march into the center of the American consciousness. The Nashville-born novelist Madison Smartt Bell told me a story about going to visit Kershaw just before he died. Though he described Kershaw as a "reptilian white supremacist," Bell was still drawn to some of his art: "The curious thing is that in spite of his truly reprehensible politics, some of the work he did was really good." Walking through the old country club turned house, you'd pass through different eras and styles and idioms as you moved from room to room, Bell explained—WPA murals, sculpture, cubist portraits—"as if you had all the periods of Picasso in one house." And Kershaw was an old acquaintance of the Bell family—he'd coached Bell's father on his junior high tennis team, but his father had never seen

Kershaw's art, something Bell sought to remedy. They arranged a visit, but when father and son arrived one day in 2010, shortly after the devastating Nashville flood, the old country club turned house looked abandoned, fenced off by chain-link eighteen feet high. On the door was a FEMA notice, the ink turned slurry from the unrelenting downpour. Had Kershaw moved and neglected to mention it? They were about to leave when Bell noticed that the sections of chain-link were not bound; they could slip through the portions of fencing. Around back, a statue of Joan of Arc leaned under an overhang and both backdoors stood ajar. No sign of Kershaw, just a cat—"a big, fat, healthy, satanic cat." Somebody was clearly feeding this cat, Bell realized, and so he poked his head in the house, calling again for Kershaw. Inside, the house was falling down. When Kershaw finally emerged, he wore only his underwear; he could not remember Bell, only his father and only from way back. Kershaw, the standard bearer for so many Neo-Confederate campaigns, died soon after. He left no descendants and no will.

That was how William Dorris wound up with so much of Kershaw's art. Upstairs in the workshop, Dorris showed Ross and me two of Kershaw's paintings that he'd informally inherited. They are both huge, both nudes—the subjects are the wives of friends. Kershaw had given one as a gift but took it back when the husband tried to fight him because of it. The bigger one is displayed on a wall of a second-floor room that, in addition to the painting, is decorated with a bed and a series of monitors displaying security feeds of the statue. The painting is maybe seven feet long, the subject sprawled across a bed, the top sheet rumpled. Behind her and out the window is an intricate landscape, not unlike the background of the Mona Lisa, except it depicts a surreal Southwest landscape. Bell was right: The painting is of a higher quality than you'd expect from looking at the Forrest statue.

After we finished our tour, Dorris's phone rang. Apparently there was a situation at the Forrest Boyhood Home, down the highway in Chapel Hill, Tennessee, maintained by the local Sons of Confederate Veterans camp. To get it up to code so they could hold weddings there, someone had installed a handrail on the back porch—a big, anachronistic no-no. Dorris told me how glad he was to get off the committee in charge of such things, but he still got called about it. A beat of silence. Then: "Now that I'm mostly blind, I just sit around and wait for God."

FIFTEEN

Same as It Ever Was

Jack Kershaw was born fifty years after the Civil War ended, but had enlisted in many of the subsequent proxy wars fought over its meaning. For Kershaw, it was a civilian struggle—the battle fields now courtrooms, classrooms, roadsides—but the aim was still the same: to maintain white supremacy as a central structuring force in American life. Call it a cold Civil War. In the months after my visit to his grotesque Forrest statue, however, I began to feel as though that cold Civil War was smoldering back to life. Hate crimes had tripled the day after Donald Trump's election and continued to occur with increased regularity in the following weeks and months. At the University of Alabama, someone wrote "Trump 2016 Kill the N------" in Sharpie on a bathroom door. I published a letter in the state's major online news outlet calling on the university to be more proactive about its toxic racial climate, and in response, I received intimidating messages and threats, some of them coming from a commentator calling himself "Bombingham." White nationalists, emboldened by the president's racist rhetoric and retweets, were reaching larger and larger audiences and offering "Sieg heils" to him. In Berkeley, far-right groups brawled with the anti-fascist group Antifa. Battles over Confederate monuments escalated, drawing similar confrontations between armed militias and black-clad Antifa members in cities such as St. Louis, Houston, and New Orleans. By the time the showrunners from the television series *Game of Thrones* announced they were working on a new project, set in a future in which the Confederacy had won the Civil War, it seemed inconceivable that their fiction could be stranger than the truth we were then living.

It was amid these hostilities that I headed back up I-65 to visit another Forrest landmark in Nashville. One that pointed to the origins of this cold Civil War and that served as a reminder that although white nationalism seemed to be reemerging, in truth it had never really gone away. One that allowed me to feel the deeper pull of the tensions now threatening to tear the country apart and that provided a reference point against which I could chart the movement of the gathering storm. So one day in the summer of 2017, I sped past Kershaw's roadside grotesquerie and pushed on another twenty exits or so, waded through the city's Downtown Loop traffic, and headed for the northwest corner of Fourth Avenue North and Church Street.

Nashville, if you haven't been there in a few years, might strike you as a city transformed. High-rise condos, neighborhoods with new names, people dressed in the hats and shirts of the local hockey team. I could tell you that Church intersects Fourth just up the hill from the honky-tonks on Broadway, but perhaps better to locate it as a ten-minute walk from the Bridgestone Arena. Though the corner here at Church and Fourth is now occupied by the twenty-story SunTrust building, it was—until a fire on Christmas Night, 1961—the location of the Maxwell House Hotel.

The former hotel's distinctive Corinthian columns have been replaced by the bank office's polished marble pillars. I cased the perimeter of the building until I finally located the historic marker I was searching for. It's laid into the last pillar on the Church Street end of the building. I had to stoop a little to read it. The marker informs that "After wartime use as barracks, hospital and prison, it was formally opened as a hotel in 1869." Seven presidents stayed there, back when it was the city's largest hotel. So, too, the sign notes, did "a host of celebrities from the world of business, politics, the arts and the military services." The reason I'm here, though, goes unmentioned on the marker. Before the hotel formally opened to the public in 1869, it made certain wings of the hotel available to guests as they were completed. And it was in one of these rooms—Room Ten, to be exact—where the recently formed Ku Klux Klan held a swearing-in ceremony in the spring of 1867. John W. Morton, the Nashville Klan's Grand Dragon (and, later, Tennessee's Secretary of State), attended the ceremony in Room Ten and included an account of the meeting as an appendix to his Civil War memoir, published in 1909. The account is written by the author Thomas Dixon, Jr., who, Morton tells his readers, "has given a vivid picture of the admission of General Forrest to the order."

As Dixon tells it: "When the rumors of the Kuklux [sic] Klan first spread over Tennessee, General Forrest was quick to see its possibilities." Forrest, back in Memphis after the war, had caught wind of the Klan and learned that Morton, his former chief of artillery, was already a member. So he headed for Nashville to seek him out. On finding Morton, "The general said: 'John, I hear this Ku Klux Klan is organized in Nashville, and I know you are in it. I want to join.'" Morton apparently deflected at first, but invited Forrest to take a buggy ride with him and administered some preliminary rites. "'That's all I can give you now,' Morton told Forrest. 'Go to Room 10 at the Maxwell House to-night and you can get all you want. Now you know how to get in.'" So it was through the entrance on Church Street. with its Corinthian columns, under the chandeliers and past the gilded mirrors hanging in the lobby, and down the corridor to Room Ten, where that night "The General was made a full-fledged clansman, and was soon elected Grand Wizard of the Invisible Empire."

It's perhaps a bit too coincidental that Forrest just happened to arrive in Nashville on the very day of the Maxwell House Hotel meeting. Another story has it that an early Klan supporter travelled to Memphis to tell Forrest of the new group, to which Forrest reportedly responded, "That's a good thing; that's a damned good thing. We can use it to keep the n——s in their place," before heading to Nashville to connect with John Morton. "The truth," Forrest biographer Jack Hurst writes, "may lie in some combination of these accounts."

THE EARLY KLAN was secretive, partial to costume, given to ceremony. Hence the hotel room. They had first formed a year earlier in Pulaski, Tennessee, seventy-five miles south of Nashville. It was, at first, only a local thing, a political stunt to buoy the spirits of the war-wrecked white citizens in a war-wrecked town. (All together now: *Palliative!*) Evenings after the war, six men—James Crowe, Frank O. McCord, Richard Reed, John C. Lester, Calvin Jones, and John Booker Kennedy—would gather at a downtown law office to complain, commiserate, and play music. There's a photo of them taken September 3, 1866, skinny in their black suits, grinning from under cocked hats, fingers fretting their musical instruments. On the image's back is the caption "Midnight Rangers." They started as a minstrel troupe with the name of an informal militia.

One night, one suggested they found an organization. The idea had legs. But what to call it? "Kukloi," one suggested, from *kuklos,* Greek for "circle," popular then as a collegiate fraternity name. Another added "Klan" to alliterate and to reference their shared Celtic heritage. Ku Klux Klan, then. This new group gave the men a sense of purpose. And they embraced it. The uniform white-sheet-and-tall-hat combo came later. It started with more color, more provocation, more like a fever dream. "Like moon men," historian Elaine Frantz Parsons calls them in *Ku-Klux: The Birth of the Klan during Reconstruction.* They wore masks with horns of stuffed fabric, bonnets repurposed as masks with drawn-on thin lips and eye slits, robes and hoods of calico, ecru, and cotton, or robes of brown linen with diamond-patterned white trim. H. A. Eastman, the Freedmen's Bureau officer in nearby Columbia, Tennessee, had them on his radar. He described their purpose as being "to annoy and intimidate the colored people." They described themselves, in the pages of the *Pulaski Citizen,* like this: "the hideous fiends of night are holding high carnival over a world that is all their own."

And soon they sought to take their show on the road. If the Klan could replicate across the South—small vigilante groups, suppressing the vote in each town, intimidating Black people and carpetbaggers, scalawags and Federal troops—the Southern white man could be more than buoyed, he could "redeem" the

South, overthrow Reconstruction's federal occupation and get back to the so-called good old days. But doing so required organization, a mission, a leader.

Which brings us back to the Maxwell House Hotel and to Nathan Bedford Forrest. That night the men present allegedly signed a sort of constitution that outlined a hierarchy: the Grand Wizard at the top, a Grand Dragon in every state, a Titan for every district, and a Gorgon for every county's Klan. They would operate in a decentralized, local way but still needed someone to catalyze the movement—a figurehead who might add some celebrity sheen to the cause. As one of the founders, James R. Crowe, later put it in a letter to the UDC historian Laura Rose, "The younger generation will never fully realize the risk we ran, and the sacrifices we made to free our beloved Southland from the hated rule of the 'Carpetbagger,' the worse negro and the home Yankee. Thank God, our work was rewarded by complete success. After the order grew to large numbers, we found it was necessary to have someone of large experience to command. We chose General N. B. Forrest . . ."

While I leaned on the DO NOT ENTER sign by the corner of the bank building where the hotel once stood, I thought again of what James Perkins, Jr., the former mayor of Selma, had told me. Same war, same general.

AFTER THAT MEETING here in downtown Nashville, Klans rode across the south. Upon seeing photographs of Richmond after the war was over and the siege had ended, more than one journalist proclaimed America an old country now that it had ruins. And if it was finally old, it could be made anew. Reconstruction, as its name suggests, sought not only to rebuild the physical landscape but also to forge a new ideological foundation—for the South and for the country. The Fourteenth Amendment would vest full citizenship to the formerly enslaved and, essentially, write the Declaration of Independence into the Constitution. It sought to cut out the sickness—the organization of American society around a false belief in white supremacy—and dispense with the palliatives. But vesting the formerly enslaved with full citizenship required a military occupation, one that was met with a fierce resistance.

"Under Forrest's control, the Ku Klux Klan became a major force of counterrevolution in Tennessee and the rest of the South," writes biographer Brian Steel Wills. Wills identifies a pattern that developed over the late 1860s: Forrest was then the president of a railroad company and often traveled across the South. He'd show up in a given town and, while there, would parley with the town's former Confederates. Wills then notes how, soon after Forrest's visit, notices about the Klan would appear in the local paper. Thousands across the South eagerly joined. There's a famous story that goes some way toward explaining why. Toward the end of the war, a formerly enslaved man encounters his old master at a Confederate prison and greets him, "Howdy Massa. Bottom rail on top, this time." The need to restore those rails to their prewar setting swelled the Klan's ranks. And so when a crew of Klansmen menaced Simon Elder, a Black landowner prosperous enough to hire some white laborers, he knew why: "I was getting too much for them."

Take, for instance, a sample case from Elder's home state of Georgia: the ten months between January to November, 1868,

when the Freedmen's Bureau reported 336 instances of violence. There were two elections during that time, for governor
in April, and for president in November. In one county, 1,144
voted Republican in the April election, by November only 116.
In another county that number went from 1,222 Republican
votes to just one. The Klan subverted Reconstruction with an
extraordinarily vicious set of tactics: they burned crops; threatened families; beat, raped, and lynched Black people and those
who wanted to include them in society. The Klan attacked an
estimated 10 percent of Black people who attended Southern state
constitutional conventions in 1867 and 1868. All told, the Klan
was responsible for thousands of murders.

In 1871, Congress opened an investigation: the Joint Select
Committee to Inquire into the Condition of the Affairs in the
Late Insurrectionary States. Their report runs thirteen volumes
and is the definitive story of the early Klan. During that investigation, Attorney General Amos Akerman and Army General
Lewis Merrill traveled to South Carolina, where a local Klan den
had reportedly killed eleven and assaulted 600. Merrill described
what he saw there as a "carnival of crime not paralleled in the
history of any civilized community."

The committee called Forrest to Washington to testify. In his
testimony, Forrest gave elusive answers, denying involvement in
or knowledge of the Klan. Asked if he took any steps to organize under the Klan's prescript, he responded, "I do not think I
am compelled to answer any question that would implicate me
in anything; I believe the law does not require that I should do
anything of the sort," and when asked who were the members of
the organization, Forrest told them it is a question he does not

wish to answer then, before asking for more time to consider his response. He would eventually describe Klan members as "worthy men who belonged to the Southern Army." In 1868, Forrest had given a newspaper interview in which he demonstrated an intimate familiarity with the group's numbers and tactics and indicated that he lent support to their cause. Asked about this interview before Congress, however, Forrest claimed he had been misquoted. Historians Paul Ashdown and Robert Caudill characterize Forrest's testimony as "a tactical masterpiece of verbal feints, dodges, assaults, and retreats," while noting that Forrest allegedly told a friend after his testimony that "I have been lying like a gentleman."

Some apologists for Forrest point to this testimony as evidence that he was "acquitted" by Congress of his role in the Klan, but Forrest wasn't on trial—he was testifying before a committee. "Our design," the committee noted, "is not to connect General Forrest with this order (the reader may form his own conclusion upon this question) but to trace its development." Still, Forrest always publicly denied his role in the Klan. Confirmed Klan members gave and endorsed accounts of Forrest's initiation, but they did so only after the fact, in 1905, when Dixon's account was published, and in 1907, when Crowe sent the letter to Rose. Laura Rose includes Crowe's letter in her book on the early Klan, a work endorsed by both the UDC and the SCV. Minor Merriwether, a close friend of Forrest's in Memphis, even admitted to being his Grand Scribe. Still, though, pinning down the exact story of Forrest's role gets murky. In preparation for my visit to the Maxwell House Hotel, I had called Elaine Frantz Parsons, the historian of the early Klan. "There's no reason to think that he wasn't" tapped as the first Grand Wizard, she told me, but there's no contemporaneous account. And although it's hard to discern his exact role (it was a secret society after all), Parsons does write that Forrest offered himself up as a figurehead.

And we do have an order from Forrest to the Klan: "General Order Number One," issued January 1869. "Every Grand Cyclops shall assemble the men of his Den and require them to destroy in his presence every article of his mask and costume and at the same time shall destroy his own," the order reads. So Forrest held sufficient authority over the group to hand down orders. It's disputed, though, what the order is actually saying. The common shorthand is that it's an order to disband the Klan—no robes means no riding—though others see it as a call to be less conspicuous in their ways and means. Biographer Brian Steel Wills argues that Forrest issued the order after the Klan grew beyond his control. The decentralized cells perhaps proved too difficult to corral from Memphis and so he'd rather be done with it, officially. A sort of resignation, then. In Thomas Dixon's account of Forrest's time in the Klan, the one John Morton endorsed and was the likely source for, he suggests that the order came because of the group's success. "The white race had redeemed six Southern States from negro rule," and, Dixon argues, with mission accomplished, Forrest "issued at once his order to disband."

"Redeemed"—that's their term to describe ex-Confederates' return to power. Having terrorized newly enfranchised freemen and Southern Republicans, the ex-Confederates retook control of Tennessee in October 1869, just ten months after Forrest's decree. Still, Klan violence continued for years in the states where Southern Democrats had yet to take back power. The Klan routinely menaced the 1870 elections in northern and central Alabama, in one instance lynching a teacher and five students of a Freedmen's School. But as ex-Confederates returned to state capitals and city halls across the states of the former Confederacy, more dens hung up their hoods. Federal troops officially withdrew in 1877 as a part of the brokered election of Rutherford B. Hayes, allowing white Southerners' return to full power and the reimposition of white supremacist rule. Reconstruction, such as it was, was over. As sociologist and activist W.E.B. Du Bois wrote, "The slave went free; stood a brief moment in the sun; then moved back again toward slavery."

STILL IN NASHVILLE, after about an hour of casing the SunTrust building, I was getting hungry, so I wandered into a chain sandwich shop across the street for lunch. While I waited for the same mediocre Reuben I could get in Tuscaloosa or in Lancaster, I thought about an idea from Parsons's book about the Klan—how, in the years after the Civil War, the consciousness of Americans shifted from an essentially local one to a more national one. The transcontinental railroad linked the nation, allowing people and information to connect at a much faster pace. And the Klan rode into that breach. On the ground, the Klan operated in secret, riding at night and under veil, but they donned conspicuous costumes so you'd know they were there, even when you didn't know who they were. They wanted to be both seen and unseen. Newspapers North and South reported their attacks; Congress investigated them. And Forrest, the figurehead in this vigilante war, didn't need to ride with any one Klan—as an idea, a symbol, he rode with them all. He could slip in and out of time and space, replicate across the South. In the years after the war that never really ended, the charging cavalry leader found the power of retreat. By lending his name, his support, his image, to the Klan, he could be everywhere and nowhere. Ten years before he died, his symbolic afterlife had begun. And, I realized, picking at my Reuben and looking out at the former Maxwell House Hotel, the threshold of that transformation was the door to Room Ten. There and not there. Everywhere and nowhere. Same war, same general.

SIXTEEN

The Resistance

Thomas Dixon, Jr. was preoccupied with Nathan Bedford Forrest throughout 1905. It was the year he wrote the account of Forrest's initiation at the Maxwell House Hotel and also the year he published his infamous novel *The Clansman*. The novel is a fictionalized portrayal of the rise of the Klan. It's set in South Carolina instead of Tennessee, but even so, Dixon felt compelled to give Forrest a shout-out in his note to the reader: "The organization was governed by the Grand Wizard Commander-in-Chief, who lived at Memphis, Tennessee." *The Clansman* is a love story that unfolds against the backdrop of "the Black Plague of Reconstruction," and depicts the Klan's rise as a heroic overthrow of corrupt, oppressive Northerners and lecherous, incompetent Black men. It's filled with noxious racist caricatures and it sold over 100,000 copies.

Dixon's story reached even larger audiences and notoriety in its subsequent forms, first as a play, then as a movie. There is a truth-is-stranger-than-fiction story about a 1908 production of the play in Memphis, a performance that Forrest's son, William, attended. "The curtain had been up but for a few minutes in the second act," the *St. Louis Post-Dispatch* reported, "when in rode 'the chief of the Ku Klux Klan.' The actor was made to resemble

Capt. Forrest's father." So startled was William Forrest that he "lean[ed] forward and topple[d] from his chair." He was having a stroke. William Forrest lay paralyzed in bed for a day before dying of a second stroke. Nathan Bedford Forrest's only son died from a cerebral hemorrhage he suffered after seeing his father depicted in a play. It was as if he had seen a ghost.

A third generation of Forrests, William's son Nathan, would get caught in *The Clansman*'s wake, too. Seven years after the play came to Memphis, the story hit the big screen, directed by D. W. Griffiths, and renamed *Birth of a Nation*. To tell Dixon's racist, romantic take on the early Klan, Griffiths pioneered new cinematic techniques such as the close-up and the cross-cut. One title card read: "The Ku Klux Klan, the organization that saved the South from the anarchy of Black rule." The film was massively popular, the first real movie blockbuster. In the first year of its release, an estimated three million New Yorkers had seen it. It was also one of the first films to be screened at the White House, reportedly prompting President Woodrow Wilson to respond, "It's like writing history with lightning. My only regret is that it is all so terribly true."

And the film also inspired a Georgia teacher named William J. Simmons to revive the Klan. He did so on Thanksgiving Day 1915, in a ceremony at Stone Mountain, under the Confederate portraits carved into the mountainside. Intrigued by the revival, Nathan Bedford Forrest, II, the late general's grandson, moved to Atlanta to serve first as the group's national secretary and later as the state's Grand Dragon. This second-era Klan would again function as a vigilante group, but they pursued slightly different aims than the first. As Simmons put it in a meeting in Georgia in 1920:

"Now let the N-----s, Catholics, Jews and all others who disdain my imperial wizardry, come out!" By the mid-1920s, the Klan had two million members nationwide, flexing political power not just in the South but in new strongholds such as Indiana and Oregon, where the governor of the latter admitted that it was really the Klan who ran the state. But soon infighting caused the Klan to fracture and lose political support. Then the IRS came after the organization for more than half a million in back taxes. Coffers shrank, influence waned, and membership declined.

The civil rights movement inspired a third rise of the Klan—an attempt to once more preserve the country's racial hierarchy in a period of upheaval. Groups like the White Knights of Mississippi and the United Klans of America, headquartered in Alabama, committed gruesome acts of terrorism in the decade between the Montgomery Bus Boycott in 1955 and the passage of the Voting Rights Act ten years later, including the infamous bombing of the 16th Street Baptist Church in Birmingham that killed four little girls. When enthusiasm waned in the Birmingham Klavern meetings, its leaders knew it could buoy spirits by screening *Birth of a Nation*.

But the legislative victories of the civil rights movement meant that the racial hierarchy that these white supremacists fought to protect was no longer law. They weren't upholding the government as it was—now they were in opposition to it. Katherine Belew writes in her book *Bring the War Home: The White Power Movement and Paramilitary America* that "Unlike previous iterations of the Ku Klux Klan and white supremacist vigilantism, the white power movement did not claim to serve the state. Instead, white power made the state its target." Leaders of this movement included men like William Luther Pierce, a white nationalist who founded the well-financed and highly organized National Alliance, and who authored the apocalyptic novel *The Turner Diaries*—the book that inspired Timothy McVeigh's 1995 bombing of the Alfred P. Murrah Federal Building in Oklahoma City. Men like Richard Girnt Butler, who founded the Aryan Nations, a neo-Nazi, white supremacist group known as the country's "first truly nationwide terrorist network." And Louis Beam, a Klansman and an associate of the Aryan Nations, whose 1992 treatise on "Leaderless Resistance" has become the MO for white supremacists and white power groups in recent decades. Beam advocated for groups to organize in cells rather than a hierarchy, connected by ideology but not by leadership. Shared objectives, separate organizations; same war, different generals. This makes them harder to infiltrate, easier to disavow, and gives their actions the appearance of lone wolf violence (as McVeigh's bombing was originally understood to be). The groups might occasionally come together for meetings like the World Congress of Aryan Nations in Idaho, but would operate independently.

The standoffs at Waco and Ruby Ridge and the bombing of the Federal Building in Oklahoma City meant that the federal government paid close attention to domestic terrorism and right-wing extremism in the 1990s. But, as Janet Reitman reports in *The New York Times*, focus shifted almost exclusively to international terror threats after 9/11. In 2007, however, the possibility of a Black president prompted the Department of Homeland Security to survey possible domestic threats posed by right-wing radicals. They found no shortage of chatter across the web—animosity was rising and factions were forming. Their work eventually became a 2009 report titled "Rightwing Extremism: Current Economic and Political Climate Fueling Resurgence in Radicalization and Recruitment." Affronted, Republican congressmen accused the Obama administration of a political "hitjob." They created such furor that the report was withdrawn just weeks later. As a result, attention to domestic extremism again diminished, even as the number of hate groups was ballooning. By 2011, the Southern Poverty Law Center reported that, for the first time, there were more than one thousand active hate groups in the United States.

Among them was the League of the South. The group had further radicalized in the years after Jack Kershaw's death. No longer did its members troll commuters with Dadaesque roadside art or sue the government for white reparations. (Wait, that's not entirely true. Every week in the spring of 2014, I would drive to a dive bar on the outskirts of Tuscaloosa with the woman who is now my wife, to drink Bud Light, eat patty melts, and fall in love. And every week we would pass under a billboard, stark white with plain black text in the center that read, simply, SECEDE. The billboard was paid for by the League of the South.) But the League had bigger, more malevolent things in mind, too. In an effort to boost membership, Michael Hill recruited more extreme white nationalists to replace the professors and artists who had left or died. This included people like Michael Tubbs, a former Green Beret who was arrested in the 1990s on federal theft and conspiracy charges for robbing two soldiers of their weapons, yelling "This is for the KKK," as he fled. Soon, the League of the South began to form paramilitary groups. The year after Kershaw's death, Hill urged members to arm themselves with everything from automatic weapons to "tools to derail trains."

With increased militancy came a harder ideology. In 2013, Hill went on the "Political Cesspool" radio show, where he declared, "We are for the survival, well-being, and independence of the Southern people," he told listeners. "And when we say 'the Southern people' we mean white Southerners. We are an ethno-nationalist movement and we want a free and independent South for our people, as our homeland."

Then came the Charleston Nine murders—what Dylann Roof hoped would be the opening salvo in a race war. Roof had been radicalized, in part, by reading far right websites, and his actions were a clear example of leaderless resistance: an independent actor tapped into a network of fellow radicals, his ideology was forged around an online campfire but his actions attributed to a lone wolf. As early as 1984, Louis Beam had created a proto-social-media network, Aryan Nations Liberty Net, to provide a digital platform for far-right cells to connect. In recent years, the ubiquity and speed of the internet had only made Beam's strategy more relevant.

Two weeks after the murders in Charleston, Michael Hill wrote on the League of the South's recently updated website that the attacks on Confederate monuments in response to Roof's violence represented "cultural genocide" against white people. It's worth pausing for a moment to consider Hill's response, as it provides some insight into the deep ties of identity to which these monuments are bound. That someone would claim, in the aftermath of an act of domestic terror committed with the explicit purpose of starting a race war, that *his* race was the one under attack, reveals the narcissism, the paranoia, the utter fragility of the white identity represented in these statues.

As the campaigns to remove Confederate monuments intensified in 2017, an idea began to spread among the far right: the possibility of moving from leaderless resistance to something more united. Pre-Wi-Fi groups like the League of the South were finding common cause with digital-natives who had taken to calling themselves the alt-right. Richard Spencer, a white nationalist and Neo-Nazi who runs a think tank, coined the term back in 2010. It's an anodyne term for a diffuse and shifting group of white nationalists, Neo-Nazis, men's-rights activists, and internet trolls, that had coalesced in 2014 in places like 4chan, Reddit, and Breitbart News, and their irony-laden internet presence charged into the mainstream of American political discourse during the 2016 presidential election. Mostly white, mostly men, mostly bitter, the alt-right generally believe America is a white, Christian nation and that the forces of multiculturalism, immigration, and political correctness are out to undermine white control of a white country. As Spencer likes to say, "Race is real, race matters, and race is the foundation of identity." Spencer, like many in the alt-right, rejects the idea that race is a social construct, and instead believe, based on debunked science, that white supremacy is a biological fact. In keeping with such beliefs, they also believe that "Radical Islamic terror" constitutes to them an existential threat, and legal immigration is the beating heart of the country's problem. They fear what they call "demographic displacement"—the census projections that by 2042, white Americans will become a minority of the population. They hold a deep fear of change, driven, more deeply, by a fear that should nonwhite people take power, they will subject white people to the same oppression and violence and alienation from power that white people have for so long practiced.

Yes, for some these grievances and paranoia stem from diminished economic prospects. This sentiment is perhaps best captured by a popular blogger's screen name: "Millennial Woes." But similar to their predecessors—men like Jack Kershaw who literally lived in a country club or Michael Hill who was a tenured professor before leaving to run the League of the South full time—the younger generation come from all classes. The millions of dollars that conspiracy theorist Mike Cernovich made from his Facebook stock did not temper his views on gender and race. Proud Boys leader Gavin McGinnis had cofounded internationally influential Vice Media, while the ascendant alt-right leader Richard Spencer's family owns thousands of acres of cotton fields in Louisiana, where they receive millions of dollars in subsidies from the federal government. This racial entitlement cuts across class lines, as it was invented to do.

And the mainstreaming of so many of the alt-right's ideas, attitudes, manners, and methods led to a novel idea: coalition building. Move from the computer to the concrete, from leaderless resistance to something more united. For so long the undertow in national politics, they were now the tide. "We've crossed the Rubicon in terms of recognition," Richard Spencer told those gathered at his National Policy Institute convention just after the 2016 presidential election. Trump, buoyed by their movement, had reached the highest echelons of power. What might they be able to do? What if they did some real-life coalition building? It seemed like it was now or never.

Instead of a meeting at a place like the Maxwell House Hotel, they found a Confederate monument to rally around.

• • •

BY EARLY 2017, Confederate monuments were a prominent theater of political war. In New Orleans, Mayor Mitch Landrieu delivered a speech on the occasion of the removal of the city's monuments—a candid, scathing analysis of the statues' meaning: "These statues are not just stone and metal. They are not just innocent remembrances of a benign history. These monuments purposefully celebrate a fictional, sanitized Confederacy; ignoring the death, ignoring the enslavement, and the terror that it actually stood for." Removing them, he said, was an effort to "Making straight what was crooked, making right what was wrong."

To the far right, those were fighting words. Companies contracted to remove the statues in New Orleans received a barrage of death threats. The *Daily Stormer*, a prominent neo-Nazi website, referred to those months of monument debate as "the summer of the black sun," deploying the approaching total eclipse as the emblem of the rise of Nazism amidst increasingly frequent and violent standoffs. Members of disparate far-right groups kept running into each other at protests in St. Louis, Gainesville, and San Antonio. Neo-Confederates gnashed teeth, brandished weapons, and shouted down anti-fascists alongside anti-government "Patriot" groups. In such close proximity, they began to feel each other out. Already that April, the League of the South, along with two other militarized far-right groups, had hosted a weekend retreat to train and organize, solidifying the bonds of what they called the Nationalist Front. Antifa groups were confronting the far right at many of these demonstrations, supplying a boogeyman and adding an urgency to the groups' possible alliances. Brad Griffin, the public relations chief for the League of the South, who uses the pseudonym Hunter Wallace, wrote on his blog that spring, "Groups and individuals who don't have a history of working together perceive a common threat now . . . The movement has always been divided over National Socialism, religion and countless other wedge issues." But, with Confederate monuments under threat, Antifa standing them down, and an opportunity to consolidate a growing political power, Griffin felt they should "organize a larger and even meaner gang."

With the so-called "hard right" united, could the broader alt-right unite, too? Many felt their fates were tied to the monuments—an alarmist symbolic logic that connected the removal of the statues to the decline of the white race. The "cultural genocide" that Hill diagnosed in 2015 had only intensified, they felt. Statue preservation was self-preservation. Their blood, their soil, their statues. For as much as they snarl about the left's constant invocations of identity politics, they, too, are practitioners of this very thing, it's just that theirs are the identity politics of the white male. From anti-PC trolls to Western Chauvinists, Neo-Confederates to Patriot militias, they all now had a stake in Confederate symbolism. Brad Griffin of the League of the South articulated the terms of alliance on Facebook after a monument protest in Houston that summer: "Patriots and Rainbow Confederates believe we can all get along. We can become a minority in our lands and somehow everything will be fine. The removal of Confederate monuments in New Orleans, San Antonio, Orlando, and St. Louis suggest otherwise." A little later in the exchange, after a commenter suggested that their removal is the will of a democratically elected government, Griffin responded, "So, it turns out that the result of a multiracial democracy and becoming a racial minority is the destruction of our monuments. Who could have predicted that?"

Soon after, Griffin appeared as a guest on the "Rebel Yell" radio show along with a relative newcomer to the alt-right, Jason Kessler, who was organizing a rally in his hometown of Charlottesville, Virginia. The Charlottesville city council had voted to remove its two Confederate statues, but a court injunction had halted the removal process. The statues in limbo, Kessler hoped to parlay the standoff into a flashpoint for the alt-right. On the show, Kessler explained that, "The number one thing is I want to destigmatize pro-white advocacy . . . I want a huge, huge crowd, and that's what we're going to have, to come out and support, not just the Lee Monument, but also white people in general, because it is our race which is under attack."

Fittingly, Kessler dubbed his event "Unite the Right." The general orders for the day encouraged everyone to bone up on the lyrics to "Dixie." And although the organizers secured permits with the city of Charlottesville with the assurance that the rally would be a peaceful assembly, a series of leaked posts from the message board used to plan the rally included tips to embed screws into hand-held flagpoles and memes about driving cars into crowds. On the list of featured guests at the event: Michael Hill. In a speech back in 2011, Hill had asked the crowd, "What will it take to get you to fight . . . what would it take to turn you into a William Wallace?" The answer for many, it turned out, was the attempted removal of a Confederate statue in a sleepy Virginia college town.

SEVENTEEN

This Is Us

On the morning of June 8, 2018, I emptied my pockets, opened my backpack for inspection, passed through the metal detector, and entered the Charlottesville General District Courthouse. I'd arrived early, about an hour before the day's docket would begin, wanting to make sure I got a seat. The courtroom was comprised of blonde-wood furniture, brick walls, drop ceilings, and a gallery already starting to fill with journalists and supporters of the defendants.

I'd arrived in town the night before and had gotten up early to retrace the routes of some of the principal characters from the rally. I was spared the shoe leather, though, as everything I was there to see lay within a quarter-mile radius. In fact, just across the alley from the courthouse stood the parking garage where, the morning of the rally, Michael Hill assembled the League of the South contingent along with the rest of the Nationalist Front. Their line, five abreast, coiled up several levels of the garage. They brandished shields, donned baseball helmets, raised the red and blue of the Confederate flag or the black-and-white cross of St. Andrews (a symbol of Southern nationalism). Michael Hill, in a black utility vest and combat boots, led them down to street-level. At his side were his chief of staff Michael Tubbs, the former

Green Beret's long gray hair tucked behind his ears, and Spencer Borum, the League's boyish Kentucky chairman, bearded and bespectacled, waving the St. Andrews flag. "Hail Virginia," Borum called to the hundreds behind. "Fix bayonets," another cried. Then Hill led them into the late-morning glare of Market Street and the awaiting battle.

It's three blocks down Market Street from the parking garage to Emancipation Park, the site of the rally. The park is a square block, situated on a raised knoll of grass, so you can only enter the park via the set of stairs at each corner. Michael Hill had marched down the center of Market Street, with the gang of Nationalist Front marchers at his back stretched out for a full city block. At the corner of the park, about twenty counterprotesters had linked arms across the entrance in anticipation of their arrival. Leading with shields and bats and the points of their flagpoles, the League charged their line. "That was when the biggest part of hell broke loose," one attendee told me. It was a wave-crash convergence of the two forces, their ranks buckling into an intimate melee of hand-to-hand combat. Tubbs put his head down and barreled into the counterprotesters. Fellow members dragged one woman down and into their line. After the initial charge, Hill reformed the line and they forced their way through the blockade, flanked by a man training his pepper-spray nozzle on the counterpro-testers. Once inside, they formed a tortoise-style shield defense on the steps into the park, Michael Hill at the top. Below: taunts and insults, bottles and rocks volleyed back and forth. Nearly fifty years to the day after Jack Kershaw orchestrated a riot over school integration, Hill leaned on his walking stick, his expres-sion placid, as he surveyed his own riotous defense of whiteness.

The vision that Hill and Kershaw laid out in the mid-nineties when they founded the League and hoisted their Forrest statue had gained such traction that, twenty years later, it landed Hill as an agent of violence at the nation's largest white supremacy rally in decades.

CASES ARE LITIGATED in Charlottesville with all parties standing at the bench, so just after 11 a.m., when Corey Long entered the courtroom, he bypassed the empty defense and prosecution tables and approached Judge Robert Downer's bench. Long wore a red shirt crossed with black suspenders, fastened to black slacks. He was facing two charges, misdemeanor assault and disorderly conduct, for two encounters that occurred just after the League of the South arrived at the park. When Long arrived at the bench, he, his attorney Jeroyd Greene, the Commonwealth prosecutor Joe Platania, and Judge Downer, all proceeded to do what so many have done in the months since the rally: hunch over a laptop to parse footage from the rally.

The footage came from a moment about half an hour after the League stormed the stairs of Emancipation Park. The ensuing battle for control of the Market Street entrance had prompted the Charlottesville police to issue an order of dispersal. On the heels of that order, the governor of Virginia declared a state of emergency—anyone remaining in the park would be arrested. Protesters and counterprotesters alike began to stream out of the park. Long had been standing at the next set of stairs down from the League's position, taking cover under a boxwood hedge. A lanky twenty-three-year-old Black man who worked as a caregiver in town, Long had arrived at the park at eight that morning.

"I just went down there to speak my mind," he explained to me, not knowing exactly what to expect, but not expecting what he found. "It was pure hatred. That's all you saw," he said, shaking his head. "It was like a horror movie." He estimates he heard the N-word fifty times as he roamed the perimeter of the park. People spat on him, threw rocks, and, at one point, a can of spray paint. Long decided to grab the can. Police had done little to intervene all morning, and his nerves were frayed. As the white nationalists left the park, they streamed past him at the foot of the stairs, and the insults continued.

"Fuck you, n-----," Richard Preston, the Imperial Wizard of the Baltimore County Klan, said to Long, getting in his face. The footage showed Long spraying the can of paint at Preston and two other men who had approached him—"Just to push them back," he testified. It was enough to turn Preston away and to force a squat man in cargo shorts to retreat up the steps. But the crush of people continued unabated, and so did the threats. So Long put a lighter to the can and sent a rope of flame up the steps to keep the men at bay. In response, the man on the steps swung his furled Confederate flag at Long. Then, the footage showed Preston double back toward Long, pull his gun, and draw a bead on Long's head. With no bullet in the chamber, Preston lowered and cocked the handgun and this time, aiming lower, fired at the ground at Long's feet, sending up a clod of dirt. Preston quickly holstered the weapon and receded into the stream of people leaving the park.

Anyone paying attention to the news at the time probably has seen a photograph of this moment. Everyone was inundated with images and videos from that day, but this one sticks out.

It's a photograph by Steve Helber, an AP photographer. In it, Long stands at the bottom right corner of the frame in a wide-set stance, one arm held out, wielding the aerosol can, the other holding the lighter. Above him on the left, the man in cargo shorts appears dumpy and timid, knees locked. His outstretched flag threatens to capsize him down the steps. The streak of flame burns dead center between them. It is a stunning photograph, full of elemental fury.

But it has also led to a charge of disorderly conduct. Jeroyd Greene, Long's attorney, argued that his client's use of the flame-thrower should be understood not as an action but as a reaction. A reaction to chaos, to a lack of police presence, to the fact that these rally goers had chosen to engage Long. "Armed with conviction, belief, and a voice," Greene maintained that Long was entitled to defend himself. Commonwealth prosecutor Joe Platania countered that his first spray—just paint, not fire—succeeded in getting the two men to stand down. Igniting the can after Preston retreated, however, provoked further retaliation and endangered all those in his immediate vicinity.

Litigation then moved to the second charge against Long, misdemeanor assault, which stemmed from an incident that took place soon after. Having avoided Preston's bullet, Long and several friends had set off down Market Street, heckling members of the League of the South who were retreating to the parking garage. This was a brief window of time that afternoon, less than two hours all told, when counterprotesters felt they had won the day. Armed, violent white supremacists from all over the country had come to Charlottesville and, without aid from police, these counterprotesters had stood them down. And all before Michael

Hill could even deliver his speech. Chants of "Whose streets? Our streets!" carried over the cobblestone. Quickly, though, that joy turned to grief and anger when James Allen Fields, Jr. drove his car into a mass of counterprotesters, injuring dozens and killing a thirty-two-year-old named Heather Heyer.

But it was in that earlier brief window of celebration that Corey Long allegedly attempted to snatch the Confederate flag carried by Harold Crews, a member of the League of the South. A game of tug of war ensued. That was when DeAndre Harris, a friend of Long's who believed that Crews was trying to spear Long with the pole, swung a flashlight toward Crews. He'd later claim that he was attempting to break the flagpole but from footage of the encounter, it appears that he instead caught Crews with a glancing blow to his head. But the swing provoked a bystander to deploy his pepper spray, causing everyone to fall back. Seeing Harris reeling, six more rally-goers pounced on him, stomping him and beating him with metal poles, signposts, and the arm of the parking garage gate. It was a vicious attack. Harris—with a fractured wrist, a concussion, and a sizeable gash on his head—got to his feet, woozy and bleeding, and managed to escape into the parking structure, where he reunited with Long. Long told me that the two hid out in one of the stairwells of the garage until the crowd dispersed.

In the span of about twenty minutes, Corey Long had stood down an Imperial Wizard of the Klan with a flamethrower and had wrestled with a member of the League of the South—back-to-back battles with latter-day Forrests come 'round again. For it, Long was embraced by the Black Panther Party and heralded by progressives online. Even *The New Yorker* commented on how the image of him with the flamethrower evoked the fire of Black liberation.

But now, ten months later, Long had to stand trial for those actions. Several members of the group who attacked Harris in the parking garage had been charged and convicted for their actions. But in an effort to revise the narrative of the day by casting themselves as the victims, members of the League of the South pressured Albemarle County officials to charge both Harris and Long. And their early efforts proved successful—both men were indeed charged. Later footage revealed that the injuries Crews alleged were caused by Harris's flashlight had more likely come from another fight that day. (Harris would later be cleared of charges.) And though Crews had at first seemed willing to pursue charges, he had not shown up for court that day. In fact, the prosecutor told the judge that he had not been able to reach Crews at all in the lead-up to the trial and so would no longer be pursuing the assault charge against Long.

That left the disorderly conduct charge to settle. Judge Downer admitted that the statute was problematic for a judge, as it requires proof of a specific intent to create disorder. In his seventeen years on the bench, Downer said, there had been only a few cases that had warranted a guilty verdict. But this was one of those times. Judge Downer sentenced Long to 360 days, suspending 340 of them. When he did, a hiss broke out from the crowd. Actions such as Long's, Judge Downer said, had "cost Charlottesville its reputation as an All-American city."

DOWNER'S COMMENTS ECHOED a trend I'd noticed in the way some people commented on the Unite the Right rally in the months since, both online and here in Charlottesville. On social media, it can often take the form of an aggrieved comment on an article or a retweet to footage from the rally, asserting that "this isn't us." Bumper stickers I saw in Charlottesville proclaim that "This is OUR town: Openness, Unity, Respect," reflecting a feeling that, because so many who attended Unite the Right were from out of town, this university town was being held responsible for attitudes cultivated in other places. It's become a modern-day Selma. And this self-righteousness makes sense. People *did* come from all over: Neo-Nazis from Indiana and Neo-Confederates from Arkansas, Proud Boys from New York and white nationalists from Ohio. But broadening the blame can't lessen any one city's share. It just implicates everyone. In that way, I think, Charlottesville has *become* an All-American city. Corey Long seemed to think so, too. Reflecting on his experience at the rally, Long told me that the rally "reminded me of stories my grandfather used to tell out in rural Virginia. Finally, it really made sense."

This *is* us. Always has been.

To wit: In 1898, Alfred Moore Waddell, a Confederate monument booster, led a mob to burn a Black newspaper office in Wilmington, North Carolina, sparking a coup to overthrow a biracial government and reinstate white supremacist rule. In 1956, Jack Kershaw, a Confederate monument booster, led a series of protests in opposition to integrated schools that sparked two days of riots and the deployment of the National Guard. And in 2017, Michael Hill, a Confederate monument booster, broke loose the biggest part of hell in Charlottesville, Virginia, when he marched a column of white nationalists down Market Street and into a melee.

The oft-quoted definition of insanity is doing the same thing over and over and expecting different results. Perhaps our

American insanity is creating and institutionalizing a false sense of racial superiority, while expecting to foster an open, democratic society. The rally, then, was a very American expression of our madness about race. From across the country, white people came to Charlottesville to assert their racial prerogative. They came to demand what, for so long, had been simply given as the palliatives of their race. But now, as the country awkwardly lurches forward, they have to ask for it. We are in a moment where some of us are finding ways to see, talk about, and begin to reckon with the inequities wrought by white supremacy, to identify the ways our notions of race have hobbled us. But it's a push and pull. These clunky steps toward another way of being makes others anxious, makes them want to pull rank, to exert their racial prerogative, maintain that hierarchy, and resist these shifts by any means necessary. To spit in the bucket, as the Agrarian Andrew Lytle would have us do.

Ironically, by violently defending the traitors who made up the Confederacy, Unite the Right expressed something essential about American whiteness—as if their Plexiglas shields were meant for us to catch our reflection in. I set out on this journey trying to better understand my country and myself through the stories of Confederate monuments. Charlottesville offered an answer, but it was an answer that our long-held insistence on white American innocence has trained us to look away from. If we white people want to move away from the America embodied in this rally, the America that would have looked so familiar to Corey Long's grandfather, we are going to have to redefine our sense of what "All-American" means, let a fuller sense of how race operates in this country temper that definition.

WHEN I GOT up from the courthouse gallery and blinked my way out into the high-noon sun, I was reminded that there were plenty in Charlottesville who did not subscribe to Judge Downer's amnesia. Representatives from several other churches, Black Lives Matter, Standing Up For Social Justice, and Congregate C'Ville were there to remind Corey Long that they saw his actions as a welcome rejection of a noxious ideology. They had packed the courtroom to support him, and now, as they waited for him on the sidewalk, they chanted the refrain that had become all too common recently, "Corey Long did nothing wrong!"

When he emerged from the courthouse, he was flanked by members of the New Black Panther Party, who were offering legal support. Long looked a little stunned by the verdict, but he briefly addressed the crowd.

"It is what it is," he said, shrugging. Then he paused. He wasn't taking questions, but one seemed to be occurring to him. "Would I do it again? Hey, you never know."

Would he again confront armed Klansmen and Neo-Confederates, these latter-day Forrests come 'round again? You never know. But it seems assured that if we continue to look away, believing this isn't us, someone will have to.

PART FOUR

Down Along with That Devil's Bones

Memphis

EIGHTEEN

A Symbol of Everything
We Are Fighting Every Day

Not three hours after James Fields drove his car into a crowd of protesters in Charlottesville, Tami Sawyer set out for Health Sciences Park in Memphis's Medical District to mourn at the foot of Nathan Bedford Forrest. Sawyer, a Memphis native in her midthirties, is a grassroots organizer and the founder of #TakeEmDown901. She spent the morning at home, staring at CNN in horror, as she followed the unfolding news from Charlottesville. She was in tears when she called her friend and fellow organizer, the Reverend Earle Fisher. They had to do something, she told him, and not just a Facebook post or a news conference. "I think we go to the space of this statue and stand in solidarity." So they put the word out and headed for the statue. Within an hour, hundreds of people had come out to join them. The impromptu rally set off a week of protests and initiated the endgame in #TakeEmDown901's campaign against Forrest.

Sawyer and Fisher have been "attached at the hip," as Rev. Fisher put it, ever since Memphis police officer Connor Schilling shot and killed nineteen-year-old Darrius Stewart during a traffic stop in 2015. "That was Memphis's Mike Brown," Fisher explained, referring to the young man shot by police in Ferguson,

Missouri, whose death catalyzed the Black Lives Matter movement. Since then Sawyer and Fisher have teamed up to tackle
issues of police violence, income inequality, voting access, and
at the forefront of their minds that day in August, Memphis's
Confederate statues.

On the south end of Health Sciences Park, the August heat at
its late-afternoon worst, Sawyer climbed the marble base of the
statue. Above her, on horseback in bronze, sat Forrest: the goatee
long; the square jaw set; his gaze impassive, alert to the middle
distance, and at 21 feet above the base, impossible to meet. The
puffed chests of horse and rider are shielded from direct light
and so have tarnished darker, spared the weathered verdigris of
the rider's sleeves and horse's haunches. To see the statue from
Sawyer's vantage—a gaze goes upward from the stirrups to the
double-breasted general's coat, to the stare into the nowhere
of the horizon—is to see a flex of intimidation. It is striking.
Unnerving. Intentional. But Sawyer was unbowed.

"What these statues do is give power to a white supremacist
movement that is reemerging and growing as we speak every
day," she told the crowd, and that the Charlottesville rally offered
clear evidence of how they intended to use that power.

The hundreds of people who came out that afternoon to
stand with Sawyer and to stand down the Forrest statue made
it the biggest rally to date of #TakeEmDown901's campaign. For
Sawyer, it was also the biggest protest she'd led in over a year—
since she organized protests in response to the police killings
of two Black men, Philando Castile in Minneapolis and Alton
Sterling in Baton Rouge, the previous summer. Now, standing
under the Forrest statue, Sawyer experienced a flashback to those

protests, to the vehicles halted by those marches, their engines revving. Then the footage from the Unite the Right rally flooded her mind, the muscle car accelerating into a crowd of people, bodies flying up and off the car like stalks of grain from a threshing machine.

Not that Sawyer was naïve about the life-and-death nature of the campaign she had undertaken—she joked, early into our conversation, about how, if I don't hear from her in a while, my next assignment would be to find out what happened to her— but still, the Unite the Right rally was a visceral reminder of the stakes. "It could have been us," Sawyer told me.

BACK IN 2015, the Memphis City Council had voted unanimously to remove the Forrest statue. But a week after the council vote, hundreds of people went to the park and celebrated Forrest's 193rd birthday. Lee Millar, the spokesman for the local Sons of Confederate Veterans troop, addressed the crowd. He listed the logistical difficulties the city still had to face in order to remove the statue and hoped the gathered group would be one of them. The Confederate caucus obliged two weeks later at the city council's next meeting, speaking against the motion to finalize the city's application to the state historical commission. Responding to the Sons of Confederate Veterans' insistence that the council cannot change history, then-Mayor A. C. Walton said, "We can't unring a bell. But how long do we have to pay fealty to it? That's what monuments represent. I'm resolved we're going to remove it." That resolve, however, was not enough to persuade the Tennessee Historical Commission, who heard and denied the appeal in late October 2016.

But something was amiss. The Heritage Protection Act, remember, was first passed in 2013, then updated in 2016 to require a supermajority of the Historical Commission to permit the removal of statues. Yes, but as Memphis city council attorney Allen Wade pointed out, while the Commission ruled on the city's request after the Act was updated, the city had applied for a waiver *before* the legislation passed. The point being that the commission had adopted the newer set of rules to evaluate an application that had been filed while the previous rules were still in place. Reavis Mitchell, the chairman of the Historical Commission, disagreed with that point of process, but still, it was a toehold toward an appeal: if the commission had adopted the wrong set of rules, their ruling could be invalidated.

When, or even if, that appeal might take place, however, remained unclear. With the city's bureaucratic efforts stalled, Tami Sawyer hit the pavement. For months, like a bad song, the image of the Forrest statue had been stuck in her head. In January 2017, when an Ohio grand jury did not return an indictment on Timothy Loehmann, the officer who killed twelve-year-old Tamir Rice, Sawyer's mind went to Forrest: "A young boy could be killed for playing with a BB gun in his local park and here in our park stands this statue of the Grand Wizard of the Ku Klux Klan." In response, she organized a "healing circle" at the foot of the statue. A healing circle, Sawyer explained, creates a place for people to talk, pray, sing, hold space—if there is anything that people need to do after one more painful reminder of whose lives matter, they can do it around others. "I just believe in the power of not sitting at home on Facebook with your anger," she said.

Sawyer is animated and outgoing, has a personality suited to organizing. When we met for espressos (double espressos, she's also very busy) at a place just up from Health Sciences Park, Sawyer was fresh off her win in the Democratic primary for county commissioner. She's bright, prone to laughter—a product of both a scathing wit and a stubborn joy. She's expressive, talks with her hands (her fingernails that day were painted a bright blue—vivid, visual punctuation marks to the story of her campaign against the city's Confederate monuments). And she's steeped in legacy of civil rights protest and is committed to carrying on that work. Sawyer's father used to be the CFO of the National Civil Rights Museum, so as a teenager, after school, she'd walk in the back door of the Lorraine Motel, where Martin Luther King, Jr. was assassinated in 1968, and where the museum is now based.

To her, the Forrest statue represented "A symbol of everything we are fighting every day," and so she was constantly reminded of it. Whenever she wrote about Memphis, she found herself referencing the statue. A week after the healing circle, she introduced Angela Davis, the legendary civil rights activist, at a benefit dinner, welcoming Davis "to a city that is 67 percent Black and 26 percent poor . . . to a city that underserves its population with inadequate transportation and underfunded, segregated education . . . to a city that profits from being the town where Dr. Martin Luther King was assassinated and claims to live out his dream, but spends money and energy protecting the statue of a man who made his fortune off the abuse and destruction of the bodies of Black men and women, Nathan Bedford Forrest."

It's maybe no surprise, then, that when she was asked at a work retreat to set an achievable goal, the answer came off the top of her head: "Remove these damn statues," she said, Historical Commission be damned.

While city officials continued to voice support for the removal of the Forrest statue (along with the city's two other Confederate statues—one of Jefferson Davis, the other of Capt. J. Harvey Mathes), there was no discernable movement on the issue. Would the city appeal the commission's ruling? Could they just go ahead and remove them anyway? When the City of New Orleans removed its Confederate statues in May 2017, Memphis city attorney Bruce McMullen was asked about the status of Memphis's own statues. "The way it's set up, it's going to be very onerous to get their approval to remove the statue," he said. To Sawyer, it seemed like the politicians were hedging, being overly deferential to the commission. A follow-up statement from the city only furthered that sense: "Our situation differs from New Orleans in that Louisiana does not have a law similar to Tennessee's." The city would proceed as the law required, but, to the outside observer, the Heritage Protection Act and the Historical Commission were constructed specifically to foreclose, or, at the very least, slow-walk any efforts toward removal.

So Sawyer forced the issue.

After the work retreat, Sawyer floated the idea on social media of a grassroots movement to remove the city's Confederate statues. Several hundred replies later, Sawyer saw that things had gotten real. Quickly. Three hundred and fifty people showed up to the first meeting that June, including city councilmen, county commissioners, a state senator, a member of hiphop group Three 6 Mafia, and William Webb, a descendant of Nathan Bedford Forrest, who told the crowd, "I want to stand here and publically state that I am for the removal of all Confederate monuments, not only here in Memphis but across the state of Tennessee."

"I was like, 'Okay, we have a *movement*,'" Sawyer said.

Through the summer—"that long summer," Sawyer laugh-groaned—the group began organizing under the hashtag #TakeEmDown901 (901 is the area code for Memphis), a reference to the New Orleans organizers, Take Em Down NOLA, who had maintained years of pressure on the city to remove their monuments. The hashtag helped coalesce online support while Sawyer slogged through July, seeing to all the unglamorous legwork a grassroots effort entails: She pushed the petition, collected and mailed statements of support to the members of the Historical Commission and the mayor, did local press spots to keep the issue percolating. During a television interview in front of the city's Jefferson Davis statue, a group of Confederate sympathizers stood behind the camera waving a Confederate flag at her.

"Take care of yourself," one man said to her after the interview.

"I stiffened, hearing a threat in his voice," Sawyer wrote of the encounter in an op-ed in the *Memphis Flyer*. "For a moment, I felt the fear which they hope will keep us in a state of inaction."

Then, in the wake of the Unite the Right rally, former skeptics of the monument debate were finally ready to admit that there was a clear connection between the statues and white supremacist violence. Almost immediately, the ranks of Sawyer's movement swelled. Students at the University of Tennessee medical school in Memphis walked out of class two days after the violence in Charlottesville, and they, too, rallied in the park. One of the medical students told the crowd that the Forrest statue is a

"direct contradiction of the oath we all take as health-care pro-
fessionals: do no harm." Forrest, he said, is harmful to the city's
and to the school's reputation. The next day, in what came to
be known as the "arrest protest," police wrestled with protesters
who were trying to cover Forrest with a bedsheet, resulting in a
surreal game of tug of war over the statue and with the arrest of
seven people, one of whom was charged with "desecration of a
venerated object." Protesters surrounded the squad cars carrying those who had been arrested, banging on the hoods of the
vehicles.

The day after, on a bluff overlooking the Mississippi River
where the statue of Confederate President Jefferson Davis stands,
Sawyer encouraged the crowd to keep pushing. Public pressure
on the city was crucial, she said. Like with Forrest Hall at MTSU,
the city's Confederate statues were safeguarded by the Tennessee
Heritage Protection Act. So protesters, she said, had to force
the issue. "The city knows what loopholes there are," Sawyer
promised.

With attendance at their protests peaking, Sawyer's group
sent a letter to Memphis mayor Jim Strickland demanding the
removal of the city's Confederate monuments. They were done
asking. "White supremacy is at an apex and must be halted
nationally and here at home," the letter read. "You said yourself
that white supremacy has no place in this city. If you truly believe
that, remove the gods from whom white supremacists draw their
strength, and take the statues down today."

The group set a deadline: April 4, 2018, the fiftieth anniversary of the assassination of Dr. Martin Luther King, Jr. It was a
fitting deadline. Half a century after King's death in Memphis,

the city remained the fourth most segregated in the US, under-performing in education and income equality—in other words, Memphis still grappled with the issues that prompted the 1968 sanitation workers strike and Dr. King's visit. And it still had a massive bronze statue honoring Nathan Bedford Forrest.

While Mayor Strickland supported the issue and had voted for their removal as a city councilman in 2015, he remained committed to following the established procedure and seemed to chafe at the pressure from TakeEmDown, dismissing the group as Facebook warriors.

Squabbling with potential allies, threats at home, murder in Charlottesville—Sawyer's long summer had become increasingly bleak. I pointed out to Sawyer that recent story of Confederate statues in Memphis is, in a way, a story of foiled attempts to remove them. When she first set the goal to remove the statues, did it really feel achievable?

"It wasn't that it necessarily felt achievable," she answered. Rather, it felt necessary. Forrest had, in Sawyer's eyes, bedeviled the city for too long, was the symbol of everything she was fighting against every day. "Achievable" wasn't the point. The statues simply had to come down. "I felt like if I were mayor, I would just take them down." But the last two mayors had supported the issue and the city council and the county commission unanimously got behind it, too. Yet still the statues stayed. And it wasn't simply due to the obstinance of the Historical Commission. This battle long predated the commission. To understand what Sawyer was up against, to understand the staying power of city's Confederate statues, it's necessary to go back to the two burials of Nathan Bedford Forrest.

NINETEEN

The Dead Bury Their Dead

Technically speaking, it's now a peninsula, but it still keeps the old name: President's Island. When the Mississippi River surrounded all eight thousand acres of land just south of downtown Memphis, it was the largest island on the great river's run, but in the late 1940s, the city dammed a section of the river between the island and the city, tethering it to the shore. So, President's Island: no longer an island, now an industrial park and port. On one of my first reporting trips to the city, I took the causeway out from South Memphis to have a look around. Two main roads, Harbor and Channel Avenues, ran me up and down the developed part of the island, past all the factories: asphalt and petroleum, solvents and steel, the mammoth GlaxoSmithKline facility and the Cargill plant's huddled silos. All this industry faces the channel, where the port is. But it's only a narrow strip carved out of the woods and floodplains that make up the rest of the island—reminders of the island's agricultural past.

When the Civil War ended, in 1865, the Freedmen's Bureau opened a camp here on the island, running a saw mill and providing refuge to 1500 formerly enslaved men and women. But after Reconstruction, the island, like so much of the South, reverted to its prewar state. In 1875, the city of Memphis leased one hundred of its jailed inmates, the majority African American, to work on a new convict-labor farm on the island. The rate: ten cents per day per inmate; the lessee: Nathan Bedford Forrest. The Thirteenth Amendment had abolished slavery for all except convicts, an allowance that became the loophole by which the country maintained what writer Douglas A. Blackmon termed "slavery by another name." Freedmen and women might be arrested on vagrancy charges—for being without work or a home, or for no reason at all—then leased out to farms to labor for the city, the state, or commercial interests like Forrest's. The labor shortages of a post-Emancipation south were addressed by essentially criminalizing Blackness. Forrest, once a major force in the second middle passage of slavery, became an early adopter of its next phase, too.

His farm on President's Island would be the last of Forrest's string of postwar business ventures. His "Negro Mart" collapsed, the men and women once held inside now emancipated; his plantations lay fallow, lost to interest owed that had accrued during the war; his two railroad ventures went belly up. So Forrest and his wife, Mary Ann, moved to President's Island, living in a cabin salvaged from their plantation. The inmates lived in a divided brick house adjacent to the Forrests. They worked from can't see to can't see, planting cotton, corn, millet, potatoes. Conditions were miserable and the fields malarial, as the Mississippi flowed over the island like green water on a ship's bow. Things got so bad that the county grand jury actually opened an investigation into the working conditions on the farm. When investigators visited, a reporter for the *Memphis Daily Appeal* tagged along and could not resist a little fawning over Forrest: "There is a magnetism in his superb presence, even in his shirt sleeves and slouch hat." But Forrest was not spared the misery of the farm. He likely caught dysentery from the river water and was soon reduced to one hundred pounds, nearly half his war weight.

Prolonged visits to therapeutic springs proved futile. Forrest told a friend around this time, "I am broke in fortune, broke in health, broke in spirit." Sensing the end, he had recently given in to his wife's pleas to attend a church service with her. The homily that Sunday came from the parable of the Wise and the Foolish Builders, and afterward, Forrest approached the pastor, the Reverend George T. Stainback, to repent, confessing that he was that man—he had built his house on sand. Before Forrest left President's Island, Rev. Stainback came to him, wanting to deliver last rites and see to his soul. But, as Stainback wrote in a Memphis newspaper after Forrest's death, when he sat by Forrest's sick bed, Forrest told him, "I want you to understand now that I feel that God has forgiven me for all." He'd found peace, he said, and wanted the Reverend to know that "Between me and . . . the face of my heavenly father, not a cloud intervenes."

As you might imagine, Forrest's late-in-life salvation is often asked to hold much water in his defense. It has always struck me as odd, though. What peace had he found? For what had he sought forgiveness? Was it really a mea culpa? Whatever he confessed or denounced, he didn't say. Whatever clouds had descended upon him in that last year on President's Island, he had managed to roll away without the services of the Reverend. Soon after the war, Jack Hurst writes in his biography of Forrest, a former officer had reminded the general that he'd promised to become a Christian once the fighting stopped. Forrest apparently looked around at the Federal troops occupying the city of Memphis and responded that there was still so much un-Christian work to be done. The evangelical's emphasis on conversion allows for the sudden and assured salvation—one can be "born again" at a moment's notice by confessing to be a sinner and pledging to seek redemption in the light of His love. Clean slate. Ask and ye shall receive. So what, then, is he actually confessing? And why did he wait for the bitter end to confess it? God only knows.

But let's, for a moment, accept the storybook version of events, the one handed down over generations as Forrest's myth grew, and say he did come to see his actions—the slave-trading, the convict leasing, the Klan promoting—as reprehensible, and renounced them before God. If all that's forgiven, then why the present-day contorting about the violence of the early Klan? Why the squinting into the sun about the legality of the slave trade? Why defend him in all these things if he himself no longer would? But, again, ideology will assemble the convenient facts and blot out the rest. If you want to love Forrest, you'll find a way to love Forrest. And look: If he got right with God, far be it from me to knock it. But back here in the material world, we can still hold him accountable for his actions, right? The American carceral system—which has under its control more Black men than were enslaved in 1850—carries on the project of convict leasing and remains shadowed by clouds that Forrest helped form, even as he claimed not to see them.

Stewing on this, I pulled my car into an empty gravel lot and trudged through some tall grass to look out at the river. It was October. Unseasonably cold. Siberian, even. Okay, not really— the temperature hovered somewhere just below 50 degrees, but

I'd lost all tolerance for the cold since moving to the South. Cold enough, anyway, to call to mind a scene from Andrew Lytle's biography of Forrest, the day he left the island, that "Cold winter's day he was brought to town by raft." Bed and beef tea were the doctor's orders, and conditions out here on the island were unbefitting the deathbed scene of a revered general. So he headed for his brother's house in town and for the unclouded face of his maker. He sat in a wheelchair, wrapped in blankets, heated bricks at his feet, as he floated back to the banks of the city. Penetrating wind flapped the robes and blankets of the fifty-five-year-old. The raft poled slowly toward the bluffs, a shiver of brick and blanket on the ice-fragged water. He would not survive the year.

A stream of visitors came to pay their respects to Forrest back in Memphis. Minor Meriwether, the close friend who claimed to be Forrest's Grand Scribe in the Klan, brought his son to see Forrest in those last days. Meriwether's summation of the visit proved prescient. As they descended the steps of the house on Union Avenue, Meriwether looked to his young child and said, "The man you just saw dying will never die."

Meriwether wasn't wrong, symbolically speaking, though Forrest did shake off the mortal coil on October 29, 1877. His first burial took place two days later—Halloween. Jefferson Davis, the president of the Confederacy, served as a pallbearer; the funeral procession stretched for nearly two miles. The mourners paid their respects in First Presbyterian then gathered graveside at Elmwood Cemetery, per his last living will and testament. And that's where he'd stay. For twenty-seven years, at least, until the city required his services again.

TWENTY

The Dead Bury Their Dead Again

In the year after Forrest's death, there came a massive outbreak of yellow fever in Memphis. Nearly half the city fled in panic, some taking refuge on President's Island. Of the twenty thousand who stayed, seventeen thousand contracted the disease, and some five thousand of these died. And the epidemic wasn't limited to the city—it spread throughout the Delta to places like Holly Springs, Mississippi, where it claimed the lives of Lizzie and James Wells, leaving their oldest child, Ida, to raise her younger siblings. So Wells dropped out of Rust College, became a certified teacher, and took the family to live with an aunt in Memphis. The course of life in the city in which they arrived had been radically changed by the outbreak. Into the void came many rural Blacks and whites from the Delta, and Irish and German immigrants in from the coastal ports. With them came both a plantation ideology and also people like Wells, who were prepared to challenge it.

Wells found work as a teacher but before long began publishing articles and essays as well. In 1884, after refusing to give up her seat on a Charleston-bound train, she was dragged from the car by three white men. She wrote about the experience for *The Living Way*, a Memphis-based weekly paper. Her article about the incident brought her attention and a platform for which to continue writing; the lawsuit she filed brought a Tennessee Supreme Court case. She soon left teaching to work for the *Memphis Free Speech*, serving as a reporter, editor, and co-owner, covering issues of racial justice.

Her rise as a journalist mirrored the rise of the Black middle class in Memphis. The hub of Black life in the city was on Beale Street—the churches, the barbers, the newspapers, the music—but other neighborhoods thrived, too. Black-owned businesses flourished in a suburb of Memphis known as the Curve, where Thomas Moss, a friend of Wells', ran the People's Grocery store. The Curve had rapidly expanded and integrated in the years after the war, and with the rise in population came Black businesses like Moss's to serve it. But this growth threatened the profits of the established white economy—folks like William Barrett, who once enjoyed a monopoly on the Curve's grocery business. But it was more than the bottom line that Moss's enterprise threatened. Free Black business people threatened and enraged a sense of power clung to by postwar white civilians. Stake your identity on the lie of racial superiority, I suppose, and you are bound to feel under constant threat.

When a fight over a game of marbles broke out between a white boy and a Black boy on the porch of the People's Grocery in early 1892, Barrett used the ensuing scuffle as a pretense to press charges against Moss. The white police force was happy to oblige. The next day, the county sheriff led a raid on the grocery. More fighting ensued, this time between armed adults, and a sheriff's deputy caught a bullet in the side. In response, the sheriff arrested Moss and two of his employees, Will Stewart and Calvin McDowell. They spent less than twelve hours in custody (and none before a judge) before a group of hooded men entered the jail, removed their hoods, and marched the three men to a waiting train car. Out beyond the city limits, a crowd waited, including white journalists informed ahead of time of what was to come. The mob lined the three men up by the train tracks and killed them with a volley of bullets. Moss's last words were reportedly, "Tell my people to go west. There is no justice for them here."

Wells's response to the murders picked up on Moss's words. Memphis was "a town which will neither protect our lives and property, nor give us a fair trial in the courts," she wrote, "but takes us out and murders us in cold blood when accused by white persons." The murders, Wells writes in her autobiography, "opened my eyes to what lynching really was: an excuse to get rid of Negroes who were acquiring wealth and property and thus keep the race terrorized and 'keep the n----- down.'" She began to investigate the nature of lynching across the South—its victims, its executioners, its provocations. In May she published another editorial, this one a survey of eight recent lynchings across the region. "Nobody in this section of the country believes the old threadbare lie that Negro men rape white women," she wrote after recounting the fates of the eight cases, calling it "that same old programme." A program to "excuse some of the most heinous crimes that ever stained the history of a country," with the South "shielding itself behind the plausible screen of defending the honor of its women."

Wells's provocations were calculated. Too much was at stake— businesses, bodies, their future prosperity, or even just survival in the city—to remain silent. In speaking out, she became one of the country's first investigative reporters, developing the methods of the field in her exposé of white supremacy. The response from white Memphis was as vitriolic as her editorial was provocative. The *Memphis Evening Scimitar*, believing the author male, responded with a threat that seemed to bear out Wells's point: "If the negroes do not apply the remedy without delay, it will be the duty of those whom he has attacked to tie the wretch who utters these calumnies to the stake at the intersection of Main and Madison Sts., brand him in the forehead with a hot iron and perform upon him a surgical operation with a pair of tailor's shears."

Undeterred, Wells published *Southern Horrors* two months later. The pamphlet presented a unified-field theory of postwar racial violence: Black success in business threatened white power, consensual interracial sex threatened white masculinity. "The whole matter is explained by the well-known opposition growing out of slavery to the progress of the race. This is crystallized in the oft-repeated slogan: 'This is a white man's country and a white man must rule.'" Frederick Douglass praised the book in a letter to Wells, writing:

> If American conscience were only half alive,
> if the American church and clergy were only half
> Christianized, if American moral sensibility were not
> hardened by persistent infliction of outrage and crime
> against colored people, a scream of horror, shame
> and indignation would rise to Heaven wherever your
> pamphlet shall be read.

Over the course of the 1890s, while Wells published work that, in Douglass's estimation, should raise a scream of shame to heaven, a group of white men in Memphis raised money to build a monument to Nathan Bedford Forrest. By the turn of the century they'd raised enough to commission the acclaimed sculptor Charles Niehaus. In 1901, Niehaus, whose studio was in Paris, came to Memphis to pore over pictures and paintings of Nathan Bedford Forrest. The monument committee managed to dig up records from Forrest's tailor and could thus produce proportions of an accuracy far beyond anything photographs could provide. Niehaus wanted the statue facing south to better catch the light in the park, which took some persuading, as it ran counter to the idea that these statues should face north—Never Retreat. Niehaus also posited that a life-size statue would appear skewed from atop a pedestal and suggested the statue be one and a half times life-size, thus more imposing and proportional when seen from below. He offered to make the alteration at his own expense. Niehaus spent three years on the design, nine months on the casting.

This statue—grand, precise, larger-than-life as it was—this statue alone would not suffice. No, they had to raise the dead, too. And so, on a November day in 1904, employees at the Hoist and Bros. hoofed it out to Elmwood Cemetery, "amid flowers wilted by the early wintry blasts," as the *Commercial Appeal* described, to dig up the general and his wife. The author of the article is careful to note how the undertakers averted their eyes from the caskets when they exhumed the bodies, as "no one wished to be sacrilegious nor to destroy their conception by a glimpse at the realistic work of time and the forces of nature and decay." The gravediggers then loaded the bodies in their wagon and clopped over to the newly christened Forrest Park, where they lowered the bodies into the base of the soon-to-be-erected monument. A small crowd looked on, including Nathan and Mary Ann's son, William, and a few schoolchildren who, the article notes, "gaped in curiosity at the informal ceremony of placing the bodies under the sod."

When spring came, they unveiled the statue. "The air was soft and throaty and Southern," the paper reported of that May afternoon in 1905, and out from the roadsters that cluttered the perimeter streets of the park and out from the streetcars, recently installed and more recently segregated, thirty thousand people poured in to catch a first glimpse of the new statue. The crowd in the park was so dense that one journalist speculated it would take a police escort to elbow one's way to the statue. Veterans of the Confederate States Army trooped up Second Avenue, doubled back and countermarched in a Confederate crosshatch. Around two thirty that afternoon, Kathleen Bradley, Forrest's eight-year-old great granddaughter, climbed the terrace and yanked at the corner of the flag to reveal the bronze below. "In bronze in the fairest of Memphis parks, with head bared and intrepid eyes directed to the land he loved so well," the *Appeal* wrote of the statue, "Gen. Forrest commands today as he did in the days of struggle and strife. . . . He sits the more supreme in the saddle to exercise an unconscious influence among the people who so honored him yesterday."

The Civil War had, by the time of the unveiling, been over for forty years, Forrest dead for twenty-seven, but still his influence was required. Memphis lawyer and Forrest monument booster

S. T. Carnes tried to reckon that interval. "The present presses hard upon the past," he said. Remembering Forrest's "daring achievements" was bittersweet, because the past had been shattered to pieces, by "new men and new ideas and new interests . . . The shadows darken about the survivors of Forrest."

Senator Thomas Battle Turley then announced that "the principles of the cause for which Forrest fought are not dead, and they will live as long as there is a drop of Anglo-Saxon blood on the face of the earth." Still less subtle, a comic in *The News-Scimitar* depicted the statue with a group of Klansmen riding behind, captioned: "Forrest again wears the shroud." The ceremony's most hyperbolic moment, though, came courtesy of John Allen Wyeth, known as the poet laureate of the Confederacy, who proclaimed Forrest the "American Mars." But, as the ceremony made clear, Forrest was the God of War for a different battle now, a battle against new men and new ideas and new interests, one that had more to do with Ida B. Wells than it did with Ulysses S. Grant.

TWENTY-ONE

The Mountaintop

On a February night in 1968, an ambulance carried Echol Cole and Robert Walker through pouring rain and past Forrest Park to John Gaston Hospital, just around the corner. Cole and Walker, two Memphis sanitation workers, had been near the end of a long shift, their clothes soiled from garbage and drenched from rain. That day, there had been a sudden, heavy downpour—a "gully washer," as they say in Memphis. Four men worked a route, but only two fit in the cab, so Cole and Walker hunched on the back. When the truck hit a pothole, a stray shovel tripped a faulty circuit, triggering the compactor and crushing the two men. Their deaths prompted city sanitation workers to unionize. "We wanted to keep our jobs but we wanted some dignity, some decency out of it," Taylor Rogers, a sanitation worker who took part in the strike, explained in a 1988 interview. They worked long hours for little pay and no hope of advancing in a segregated system that kept 80 percent of the Black labor force in unskilled jobs. But Mayor Henry Loeb—a newly elected, old-school segregationist— refused to acknowledge, let alone negotiate with, the union. So on February 12, 1,300 sanitation workers marched to City Hall. "We decided that if you keep your back bent somebody can ride it," Rogers said, "But if you stand up they have to get off your back."

Dr. Martin Luther King, Jr. came to Memphis two months later, on March 28, to lend support to the sanitation workers' strike. He was then in the midst of marshaling his Poor People's Campaign, a crusade for economic justice across racial lines that would march a mule train from Marks, Mississippi, to Washington D.C. "It didn't cost the nation one penny to integrate lunch counters. It didn't cost the nation one penny to guarantee the right to vote," King said in a speech early in 1968. "But now we are dealing with issues that cannot be solved without the nation spending billions of dollars and undergoing a radical redistribution of economic power." Rev. James Lawson, an old friend of King's then helping to lead the sanitation workers strike in Memphis, told King he'd be hard-pressed to find a "more potent juncture of poverty and race" than the Memphis strike.

That year, *Time* magazine referred to the city as "a decaying Mississippi River town," but it was also known as the Plantation City. For the first half of the twentieth century, Memphis politics was a machine assembled, owned, and operated by E. H. Crump. He served as mayor from 1908 to 1916 and afterward pulled the levers from beyond the reach of the voting public. Crump named Klan leader Cliff Davis chief of police, then to a thirteen-term congressional seat. The police "functioned like Klansmen in blue uniforms," as author Michael K. Honey writes in his book on the sanitation strike, *Going Down Jericho Road*. Likewise, Crump and Loeb were against organized labor: "n----- unionism," Crump called it. But the city still drew Black people looking to escape the violence and even more drastic poverty found in the rural parts of the region. The so-called "Delta flow" kept the vibrancy of Beale Street, its music, its industry, its opportunity, shining with sufficient wattage. And yet, in 1953, the median income of Black families was $1,348, compared to $3,085 for whites. Black sanitation workers made $1.04 an hour—a forty-hour week's pay that totaled less than the welfare minimum. Thus, their strike was taking on a power system that, for the entire century since the Civil War, had systematically exploited Black laborers.

King first delivered a speech at the Mason Temple to a crowd packed up to, and perching on, the rafters, then led a march down Beale Street. But the march turned violent. Younger activists in Memphis, who did not subscribe to the Kingian tactics of non-violence, began throwing bricks through storefront windows. In response, police gassed, clubbed, and arrested marchers, three hundred in all. One police officer cornered an unarmed sixteen-year-old in a stairwell and killed him with a shotgun at close range. It was the first time an SCLC march had turned violent of its own doing.

Though the Poor People's Campaign was sputtering and sorely needed King's shoulder at its wheel, he felt he had to redeem the strike as well as the reputation of his movement. So a week later, he returned to Memphis. In a speech that came to be known as the "Mountaintop Speech," King remembered aloud how he'd been a sneeze away from death when he was stabbed in 1958 and recounted all the questions he'd heard since arriving in Memphis, people asking if he worried what "some of our sick white brothers" might do to him. No matter. "I've been to the mountaintop," he said. "I've seen the promised land." He ended by reciting the Battle Hymn of the Republic, that old war's battle cry.

The next evening, James Earl Ray, one of those "sick white brothers," in his room at a boarding house across from the

Lorraine Motel, tucked his Remington rifle under his shirt and headed for the shared second-floor bathroom. Across the street, Dr. King leaned over the balcony of the motel to request a song at that night's meeting. Then Ray unlatched the window, looked down the scope, and pulled the trigger. Just two months after Echol Cole and Robert Walker were killed, Dr. King was also pronounced dead in the John Gaston hospital, half a block from where the bronze Forrest stood.

TWENTY-TWO

A Preponderance of Goodwill

For over a century now, the Forrest statue has been a towering bronze magnetic needle on the city's compass of race and memory. Decisions about who is remembered, who matters, what Memphis should stand for, and, literally, who should stand for the city, are often measured against the statue. So many Lost Causers, civil rights activists, recalcitrant historians, and politicians of every stripe have spun into its orbit. In the years after King's death, the debate over Forrest's statue grew more heated, the critiques and defenses more pointed. In the eighties, the statue was spray painted with the letters *KKK*, and when the city used a sandblaster to remove the graffiti, they took the statue's verdigris with it. The acclaimed novelist and historian Shelby Foote, long besotted with Forrest, who he called "one of the most attractive men to ever walk through the pages of history," was hopping mad, complaining that his revered general now looked like a Hershey Bar. In 2013, when the city voted to rename Forrest Park the more anodyne Health Sciences Park, the Klan marched through town. A few years later, in an effort to hasten the city to remove the statue, a group of activists dug up a few inches of grass from around the statue, prompting one man to drive across the state with a patch of sod from his own yard to replace the divot.

"[Forrest] gives us a language in which we can argue about other things—political power-sharing, affirmative action, civil rights, equal opportunity, a host of issues that haven't been settled—while speaking about him," Michael Kelley, a columnist for the *Commercial Appeal*, noted in 2005, on the centennial anniversary of the statue's dedication. The conversation might change, but the tensions, and the setting, remained. Nearly every time I've visited the statue, there has been a police car parked on the grass, just as each subsequent state-sanctioned killing of Black Americans is likely to bring another round of graffiti or protest to the statue. Same war, same general.

And then, in the fall of 2017, there arose a new battlefield in that old war: Athens, Tennessee. The City of Memphis had successfully argued that because the Historical Commission had not properly adopted the rules of the Heritage Protection Act, their ruling was thus void. The commission granted the city another hearing on the fate of the Forrest statue.

On an overcast October Friday in 2017, the Tennessee Historical Commission came to order on the bottom floor of the McMinn County Living Heritage Museum in Athens, a small town located about 380 miles from Memphis down I-40. On the docket once more was the waiver application to remove the Forrest statue. The meeting coincided with a quilting exhibition, and the commissioners, under drop-ceiling halogens and flanked by star-block and patchwork-patterned quilts, heard nearly two hours of testimony and debate about Forrest.

Tami Sawyer and two friends drove in from Memphis to testify—an early-morning, six-hour trek that, just two months after the violence in Charlottesville, had her nervously checking her rearview mirror. "Knowing that people know what you are going for, we could have been tailed," she said. "We played music and laughed and joked but it was tense." As she pulled in, however, she realized the tragedy had already returned as farce. On the sidewalk in front of the museum, H. K. Edgerton, a Black man in the gray of the Confederacy, waved a large Confederate flag at the passing cars.

"We were like: Fuck. Okay. This is what this is going to be," Sawyer remembers thinking as she arrived and saw Edgerton.

The crowd was standing room only, the chairs arranged in an L-shape around the conference table: a contingent of Confederates to the left; a contingent of Memphis politicians and activists on the right. Testifying to the commission, Mayor Jim Strickland noted: "We must understand and come to terms with why this statue exists in the first place . . . It's a monument to Jim Crow." He circulated a comic published when the statue was first dedicated, depicting Forrest in Klan regalia. Then Sawyer addressed the commission: "We demand that immediate action is taken. These statues can no longer stand and represent inaccurate history." When she called Forrest a rapist and murderer, the crowd to her left hissed. "I felt like I was in Harry Potter," she told me, referencing the "Parseltongues" who can speak to snakes.

Speaking in defense of the statue, Memphis public school teacher Elizabeth Adams warned that "next they'll want to remove the crosses from our churches," while Edgerton referred to Sawyer as "that girl" and told of how benevolent a slave-trader Forrest was. Several men on the left side of the room stood to salute Edgerton when he finished speaking.

Finally, at the request of Keith Norman, a commission representative from west Tennessee, the council voted. "I held out hope that objective minds could see in a city that is 63 percent African American, and the statue erected with a clear intention of intimidating these people and on the eve of the anniversary of Martin Luther King's assassination in that city," Rev. Norman told me after the meeting, "that a preponderance of goodwill" among his fellow commissioners would prevail and they would grant a waiver.

The council voted: the statue stayed.

"I approached it with a sense of purity that was a little too naïve," Norman reflected. Forrest "behaved or associated with things that were atrocious to people of color and we need to recognize that." Alas, Norman said, "the evidence and hopes and cries of the people fell on deaf ears."

After the meeting, I walked out with Sawyer, past all the hanging quilts. Sawyer was exhausted by the day's travel and testimony, frustrated by the ruling, weary of the theatrics—a "shit show," she called it.

"Stay Black!" she called to Edgerton, who was back to billowing his flag on the side of the road, before she climbed into her car for the return journey to Memphis, where that night she staged a die-in at the entrance to the FedEx Forum before the Grizzlies game.

TWENTY-THREE

Remember Fort Pillow

A few weeks after the Historical Commission's meeting in Athens, I headed back to Memphis. Because the statue had once more been granted reprieve, I decided, on this trip, to visit another star in the constellation of Forrest's memory—one more distant and diminished, but no less consequential. I headed out to the Austin Peay Highway and drove north until WEVL (that hodgepodge of blues and soul and country that is a lone bright spot of these long drives with a broken CD player) turned to static. Near Henning, I tracked east, back toward the Mississippi River on a county road, under a long stretch of oaks that reached across the road to tunnel me in shade, then past the cannon at the gate of Fort Pillow State Historic Park.

The park sits on a bluff above the Mississippi River's tightest turn. The fort once stood directly above the water, allowing soldiers to fire on the boats below, but the river, ever-shifting, has now moved two miles west, away from the fort. To get a sense of this slipperiness, call up a composite map of the river over the years—it will look like snakes twisted on a staff down the center of the country. And like the river's meander, the park sits on a shifting ground of memory, offering no conclusive answer as to how one should remember the battle that took place here in April 1864.

By then three years into the war, Forrest struck camp in northern Mississippi and headed north in need of men and supplies. Twice in the past year alone, Forrest had scoured the area around western Tennessee in search of more recruits and provisions. "There is a Federal force of 500 or 600 at Fort Pillow," Forrest wrote in a letter, "which I shall attend to in a day or two, as they have horses and supplies which we need."

Fort Pillow was fronted by three lines of trenches extending outward in semicircles a half-mile into the forest. Neither a strategic hold nor a well-stocked one, the fort was built by Confederates, then abandoned, taken by the Union, but then ordered closed. Still, in April 1864, a regiment of the Tennessee Cavalry (known as Tennessee Tories for fighting for the Union) and two divisions of the United States Colored Troops (USCT) cooled their heels at the fort.

Black soldiers had been serving in the Union Army for over a year by then. Frederick Douglass had successfully lobbied President Lincoln to acknowledge that African Americans were a crucial fighting force and should not only be emancipated but allowed to fight. The Emancipation Proclamation of January 1, 1863, in addition to freeing those in slavery in the rebelling states, also called for the enlistment of freedmen in the Union Army. In response, the Confederacy passed a law that categorized all Black soldiers as runaway slaves and called for Confederates to treat them with "full and ample retaliation." Black soldiers fighting for the Union struck at the heart of their whole theory of white supremacy. White people had justified slavery by convincing themselves that Black people were subhuman and thus better off—content, even—under the rule of white masters. Former slaves taking up arms against the Confederacy flew in the face of everything they believed about their cause, about their way of life, and about themselves. As one Confederate put it, "You cannot make soldiers of slaves, or slaves of soldiers. The day you make a soldier of them is the beginning of the end of the Revolution."

Forrest's troops had yet to meet United States Colored Troops regiments in battle when they arrived at Fort Pillow on the morning of April 12, 1864. But they came spoiling for a fight. After two hours of reconnoitering and sharpshooters' fire, Forrest had the fort surrounded. He sent a truce flag and a note calling for surrender, but, perhaps hedging against what he suspected his men were capable of, he added, "Should my demand be refused, I cannot be responsible for the fate of your command."

The note back to Forrest read: "I will not surrender." So Forrest nodded to the bugler and the Confederates charged. The fighting lasted less than an hour, but the toll was enormous. Confederates routed the federal troops almost immediately. Some fled down the steep bluff to the banks of the river; many did not make it. Of the nearly six hundred Union soldiers at Fort Pillow, almost half were killed. The numbers make clear the racial motivations of the fight: Confederates killed 31 percent of men in white units, 65 percent of the US Colored Troops. Conversely, only 58 Black soldiers (some of them recognizing Forrest from his slave jail in Memphis) marched out of the fort as prisoners, compared with 168 white soldiers. Survivors wrote of Confederates shouting, "Goddamn you, you're fighting against your master," to the Black soldiers and, to the white soldiers, "You'll fight with the n-----s again, will you?" And they fought past surrender. Confederate soldier Achilles V. Clark wrote in a letter to his sisters two days later, "The poor, deluded negroes would run up to our men, fall upon their knees, and with uplifted hands scream for mercy, but they were ordered to their feet and then shot down." But Forrest himself penned the most indelible image of the battle in his report the day after. "The river was dyed with the blood of the slaughtered for 200 yards," he wrote. "It is hoped that these facts will demonstrate to the Northern people that negro soldiers cannot cope with Southerners."

Historians to this day debate Forrest's culpability in the massacre—whether he ordered it, permitted it, or stopped it from going further. He had positioned himself with the sharpshooters firing on the boats below, but there are reports from both sides of the battle that have soldiers shouting that Forrest had ordered the slaughter, for the men to be "shot down like dogs." Confederate soldiers might have embellished their general's orders, though, eager for a pretense to set upon men they saw as property. Others report Forrest ordering the ceasefire. "If it hadn't been for Forrest," Samuel Green, a Black artilleryman, wrote, "none of us would be alive today." But that order to stop the massacre would have come only after over two hundred soldiers, mostly Black, had been killed. And his report conveyed his sense of the battle's meaning, that Black soldiers were no match for him. Still, there's enough gray area for his admirers to find reason to let him off the hook, enough contextual evidence to think him guilty. Like so much with Forrest's legacy, what you see in this battlefield of memory depends on where you stand.

The way the battle is presented today at Fort Pillow State Historic Park reinforces that doubt. To me, Fort Pillow is about one thing: the racialized killing on April 12, 1864. But the museum, a dank building carved into the hill about two miles into the park, devotes as much attention to the various iterations of howitzer cannons and Confederate battle flags in the fort as it does to the events of April 12. Even the short video about the battle is at pains to point out that the question of a massacre "turns on what was fair game and what was not," while emphasizing its utility as propaganda for the Union. The video concludes: "Although the whole truth will never be known, the events of April 12 forever changed how war was fought." There is no mention of Forrest's line about the river running red with blood, about his professed belief in the inferiority of Black people. When, in the remaining year of the war, Black soldiers charged into battle, crying "Remember Fort Pillow!" they likely did not intend to call to mind the games of euchre played in the fort. And yet that is what a visit to the museum invites you to remember. It's on this spot that more than one hundred Black soldiers were slaughtered, but the ground is not hallowed.

IT'S ANOTHER TWO-MILE hike from the museum to the rebuilt fortifications on the edge of the bluff. I set off in the heat of an Indian summer afternoon, the woods smelling the way I imagine honeysuckle would if you microwaved it. The mile markers, done in neon colors, featured motivational workout quotes: "You don't have to go fast; just go." You would have no sense that you were on a trail heading for the site of a Civil War massacre.

But, I suppose, that is the point. While the park offers only half an answer to what happened here on that April day in 1864, I realized that it poses another, related question. It asks you what country you want to live in. You could spend whole days in this park barbecuing, fishing, strolling through the butterfly garden, hiking on this trail, and never be reminded that you were doing it on the grounds of a racial massacre. It's like one big coping mechanism for the horrors of America's past, laid out as a state park.

As I hiked up the bluff, I recited some lines of an Adrienne Rich poem I was trying to commit to memory. "What Kind of Times Are These" starts out bucolic, telling of an old place out in the woods, but soon turns to dread. "This is not somewhere else but here, / our country moving closer to its own truth and dread, / its own ways of making people disappear."

The trail climbed high along the ridge and then reached the fortifications—a tall wooden wall with wildflowers growing at its top. The trail deposits you behind the walls, as if you were there to wait for the breach. One Confederate, in a letter after the battle, noted how "their fort turned out to be a great slaughter pen." That's where you arrive.

I did a lap of the breastwork. There was a ditch on the outside of the wall—extra protection, I figured, like a moat or something. Not so. A sign I later found let me know that it was once a mass grave for dead Union soldiers before they were interred at the national cemetery in Memphis. I sat on a bench at the top of the bluff and read the end of Rich's poem, when the poet refuses to tell you where this place of American dread is, because she already knows who wants to make it disappear. So why say anything at all? "Because in times like these / to have you listen at all, it's necessary / to talk about trees."

It felt like a desecration to even be here. It felt necessary to talk about the trees.

I thought for a while about the oaks and the pines and about which country I wanted to live in: that foreign country of the past, or the familiar one of forgetting and grilling and hiking and traipsing across unhallowed ground.

TWENTY-FOUR

The Weight

On the morning of December 20, 2017, Tami Sawyer could barely speak. The night before, her family had to cancel her father's birthday dinner because Sawyer had laryngitis, her brother the flu. But, "dead in bed," that day she got a call from a confidant in city politics, telling her: The statues are coming down. Tonight. Go to the city council meeting, they told her, with an ear out for a certain docket number.

She dressed quickly, threw on a coat, dashed off texts to friends telling them to head to the statue. "I'm gonna go to city hall," she wrote. "Watch for movement."

Could this really be it? She had read whisperings on social media that a plot was afoot but, well, that was social media. This source, though, this felt like the real thing. On the way downtown she picked up a friend, who sat in the car, engine running, while Sawyer headed into City Hall's mid-century honeycomb of concrete and glass.

The meeting that night had come about after a chance meeting at a preseason Grizzlies basketball game. Van Turner Jr., a county commissioner and lawyer, a dapper man prone to bow ties and striped shirts, bumped into City Attorney Bruce McMullen in the stands of the FedEx Forum and, as so often was the case that year in Memphis, the two chatted about the city's Confederate monuments. Even Memphis Grizzlies coach David Fizdale had weighed in, saying, "I'm not even saying tear them up and melt them down. Put them in their proper context in history. Their proper context is in a civil rights museum, where you could put them in context and talk about how awful they were." The county commission was about to vote on the issue, and would be unanimously offering support to the city in advance of their hearing with the Historical Commission. It was there in the stands at the FedExForum that McMullen first floated an idea to Turner. It was provisional at first, as the city was still hoping to resolve the issue through the state's established channels, but given that the Historical Commission had already denied the city once, and with the MLK50 anniversary approaching, they needed alternatives. And they'd found one in the phrasing of the Heritage Protection Act. The law prevented the removal of monuments on public property, yes, but what if the city sold the statues to a private nonprofit, who could then remove the statues, unencumbered by the law? So, McMullen asked, might Turner be interested in buying a few city parks?

"[City government] knew litigation would ensue, so they wanted someone used to the court system," Turner explained to me. They also knew that, given the violent climate surrounding the monuments, it was not a decision to be made lightly. Check with your family, check with your colleagues, McMullen told Turner, and get back to me.

By the time the Historical Commission denied the city's appeal in October 2017, Turner had made up his mind: He was in. When he got the go-ahead, Turner filed for nonprofit status for a new organization, Memphis Greenspace, then began raising money. There was still a possibility of another appeal, on the grounds that perhaps the statue would be considered a historical monument, not a war memorial. But by late November, frustrated by court delays for mediation and appeal, McMullen drew up the paperwork for the sale. Then, the city council had to pass legislation that allowed them to sell property under market value. Check. And finally, on Wednesday, December 20, the last day before the state's legislative session began (when the state senate might close the loophole the city hoped to thread), a nondescript item on the docket came up for a vote.

"If you were just sitting there, you would have thought they just voted on bathroom breaks," Sawyer said. The council, without announcing the contents of the ordinance, proceeded to vote on the issue. This was the docket item Sawyer had been told to watch for. And, in a sleight of hand that would outrage the monuments' supporters, the ordinance passed. The city sold Health Sciences Park and Memphis Park to Greenspace for $1,000 each.

It was on. McMullen ran upstairs to get Mayor Strickland's signature, Sawyer ran downstairs to the car waiting to take her to the Forrest statue. Van Turner was already there, waiting to meet the removal crew under the statue.

"I was filled with anxiety," Turner told me, knowing that at any moment a judge's injunction or a misstep with the removal could jeopardize the whole plan. Instead, it was members of #TakeEmDown901 and the local media who flocked to the south end of the park. Not long after, police descended as well, clearing the park, closing Union Avenue, and sending everyone who wasn't an elected official—media and spectators alike—to wait in the parking lot of the Office Depot across the street. "It was an emotional rollercoaster," Pastor Earle Fisher told me. He had to cut short a dinner out with his wife to get to the park—he wasn't going to miss this. Once he saw the police set up a barricade and the cranes roll in, he thought, "Okay, any minute now. And then any minute now turns into thirty minutes turns into forty-five minutes to an hour."

Finally, at 9:01 (the city's area code, a little symbolic flourish from Turner), it was time. The final strap was ratcheted into place. The crane clanked into gear. The statue wobbled as the slack caught and, bathed in the blue light of the police cruisers, lifted from the pedestal. For several minutes, the bronze Forrest on horseback hovered in the air, swaying gently above the marble base, above the graves of Forrest and his wife, above the activists and journalists below.

"It was just elation," Turner told me. He thought of his father, who grew up in the city when it was illegal for him, as an African American, to enter the park, and whose birthday it was that day. He thought also of his grandmother, who lived in Sunflower County, Mississippi. "I remember as a child down in Mississippi, any time she talked about white folks, she would whisper as if they were in the room," he told me, describing the "mental weigh down" that came with growing up in fear of the white power that this statue represented, where you could be lynched for just saying the wrong thing, where you knew people who had been lynched. "It meant a lot, mentally, for people who grew up in that history," Turner said. And now two yellow nylon straps—one just in front and one just behind Forrest's saddle—held that weight, all that bronze and all those anguished memories and all that tortured forgetting, lifted it up into the blue light above the park, for all to see, and then set it down on the bed of the tractor trailer below.

"There was a level of shock and awe," Pastor Fisher told me, speaking of the mood in the crowd across the street. For so long, so many people, so many generations, had tried to get that statue down. And now, finally, they had succeeded. (Statues of Jefferson Davis and Capt. J. Harvey Mathes, in another park now owned by Memphis Greenspace, were also removed that night.) "Symbols matter," he told me. "For us to have those things removed, I think articulates to us that other things are possible. That a more equitable city and a more equitable county and a more equitable state and country is possible."

As the tractor took the statue to a police storage unit on the outskirts of town, politicians headed across Union Avenue to address the media, describing how the city maneuvered to finally get the statue down. Noting a conspicuous omission, many of the gathered spectators began chanting, "Say her name! Say her name!" Obliging, somewhat sheepishly, one councilman thanked the grassroots efforts of people like Tami Sawyer.

Shelby county commissioner Reginald Milton came across the street next and reached out a hand to Sawyer, who went to shake it. Instead, he took her by the arm and led her across the street to the park. "Being a community organizer, I know people behind the scenes don't get the opportunity to get recognition for their work," Milton told me, but as an elected official he had the requisite clearance to enter the park and, knowing how instrumental Sawyer was, wanted to give her the moment.

"We've been protesting there forever," Sawyer said, but that night, crossing Union Avenue at Manassas, "[it] felt like I was crossing the ocean. It felt so big. And I've dodged traffic crossing that street, I've done a million interviews there. It never felt so wide."

"This is your moment," Milton told her as he shepherded her past the blockade. "You did this. You deserve to be across this street."

Sawyer ducked under the police tape, climbed onto the marble base, turned to face the crowd across the street, and raised her fist.

We did it, she remembers thinking. *Nathan Bedford Forrest rides no more.*

TWENTY-FIVE

"Yeah But . . ."

F our months after the statue came down, I met Lee Millar at the foot of the statue's former home. Chain-link fence hemmed the now-empty pedestal on the south end of an otherwise bustling Health Sciences Park. Lunch-hour joggers in neon Techwick and nurses and doctors in pastel scrubs lapped the park. The outer ring of oak trees swayed in a stiff breeze, the cherry tree at center unfurled in full bloom. Millar is the spokesman for Camp 215 of the Sons of Confederate Veterans, the N.B. Forrest troop, and he is a descendant of the general as well; Forrest's paternal grandmother was his great-great-great-grandmother. Millar looked to be in his fifties or maybe early sixties. A white goatee framed his narrow face. He sounds a little like Buddy Garrity in *Friday Night Lights* and was similarly animated.

At home that night in December, he told me, his phone began to ring. And ring. And ring. "I got a call from a friend who was parked over there," he said, pointing down the street from where we stood. His friend had had a meeting in a nearby building and saw the police cars roll in to close the park. "So he called me up and said it's happening tonight. They're gonna steal the statues." So Millar started making calls, too, desperate to reach a judge, to get an injunction or a restraining order. But no one picked up. "You just don't get help here."

Millar was upset but not taken totally by surprise. "We knew the city council and the mayor wanted to remove the statues." But the secret amendment? That irked him. "You can't just take them," he said.

The next morning, chain-link fencing already surrounded the empty pedestal, but Millar hopped it to pay his respects to his ancestor buried beneath. Soon city police arrived to ask him to leave—he was now trespassing on private property.

Millar seemed confident, though, that the statues would return. On behalf of the Sons of Confederate Veterans and the Forrest family, he has helped file two separate suits against the city and Greenspace, which he calls a "sham nonprofit"—one in civil court, the other in criminal.

The injunctions haven't prevented Greenspace from hosting a series of events in the park, events that Van Turner hopes will establish a more inclusive space. Even as Millar and I spoke, a dozen people met in a patch of grass between Union Avenue and the concrete pedestal where we stood, rolled out their yoga mats, and began a series of sun salutations—the first in a new series of lunch-hour classes Turner has organized.

Millar told me that his parents didn't emphasize their Confederate heritage growing up and told him about his ancestry only when he developed an interest in the Civil War as a teenager. Climbing on the cannons during a class trip to Shiloh laid the bait; studying the war in junior high hooked him. It was only then that his parents told him, oh by the way, you're descended from John Singleton Mosby, a cavalry leader known as the Gray Ghost, and more distantly, from General Forrest.

When I pointed out the yoga class to Millar, visible just over his shoulder, and described Greenspace's effort to make the park feel more inclusive, he told me about a conversation he'd once had with a Black woman who didn't mind the statue. He then suggested that anyone who felt excluded by the statue suffered from a "mental handicap." Forrest was a Tennessean, he said, a Memphian, and revered by millions. "You should never tear down history. You should always add to it."

But the monument went up in 1905, I said. Didn't the statue say as much about the time it went up—the Jim Crow era—as it did the moment it sought to commemorate? But Millar wouldn't hear it. He insisted that the statue is about the war, plain and simple. The South just didn't have the money to do it earlier. "It had nothing to do with white supremacy, it had nothing to do with Jim Crow laws, it had nothing to do with racism." If they were putting it up because of white supremacy, no one would have stopped them from saying so, he insisted.

I tried another tack, this one from the Civil War era: Confederate Vice President Alexander Stephens said explicitly that slavery was the cornerstone of the Confederacy and thus the cornerstone of the war.

"Yeah, I feel that opinion is wrong, too. He's just one man."

When I asked if he could concede that his opponents had any points to make, he told me that he attributed the disagreement to people being "so severely uneducated" about Forrest. "They say he was a slave owner. Well big deal, so were eleven of the first thirteen presidents." He was a slave trader, sure, but it was an accepted thing back then.

"Well it wasn't accepted by everyone, surely," I said.

"It was tolerated. . . . You can't blame him for that because he was just in business." Besides, Millar said, he took good care of his slaves, never selling to anybody he felt was bad.

I grimaced and Millar cut short his next line, telling me to go ahead. I said that I was trying to put myself in the position of being enslaved and thought that there would be no such thing as a good slave owner.

"Well, you can say that today, but of course there were a lot of free Blacks then, too. But slavery was just one of those things," he said, before embarking on a lengthy explanation about how enslaved people were able to work extra hours, for pay, to make money to buy their freedom. "There were," as he put it, "avenues out of it."

And Unite the Right? Where open, avowed white supremacists defended Confederate statues explicitly because they felt they aligned with their beliefs? That march could have been at "a bus stop," he insisted. "The white supremacists used that issue as an excuse because Black Lives Matter were trying to take down the Robert E. Lee statue." In his view, it was just something, anything, to rally around.

Feeling like we were coming to the end of our conversation, I ran a theory about ideology by Millar. Was there a sort of "cafeteria Catholicism"—the picking and choosing parts of the faith that align with your worldview and discarding the rest—when it came to Forrest? "I think that happens in any case with any history. You want to remember the stuff that sinks into you and is significant to you." And for Millar, Forrest meant so many positive things, and yet his critics only wanted to talk about the negatives. So, he said, there will always be supporters who want to say "Yeah but . . ."

I was struck by Millar's framework—the contrarian impulse in Forrest's defense, it made sense. *Yeah but . . . it was legal. Yeah but . . . he's only one man.* As I walked back across the park at the end of our conversation, I wondered if, for Millar, this was all part of the fun, a kind of historical trolling. He's our guy, the thinking seems to go. We love him. If you want to hate him, fine, but you can't make me. And, in fact, the more you hate him, and the more you try to guilt me or shame me into renouncing him, the more joy I'll take in loving him.

NATURALLY, LEE MILLAR and his SCV troop were not the only ones enraged by the city's removal of the Forrest monument. In retaliation, the Republican-controlled Tennessee legislature revoked $250,000 in funding the state had earmarked for the city's bicentennial celebration slated for 2019.

"We helped that," said Billy Helton, the thirty-something leader of the Hiwaymen and Confederate 901 (who also goes by "Billy Sessions"). The Hiwaymen are a group of right-wing protesters who formed during the monument protests in New Orleans and who attended the Charlottesville Unite the Right rally. "We travel. We stand up for what's right and what needs to be defended," he explained. That list includes the Bundys, the Second Amendment, and, more recently, Confederate monuments. History needs to stay, Helton told me, good or bad.

The Unite the Right rally, which Helton attended, "built a fire in us," he told me. The removal of the Forrest statue only fanned the flame. So, two weeks after the statue came down, Helton, who lives in Scott County, Arkansas, organized a caravan around the city of Memphis, dubbing it Confederate 901.

"We sent a message to the Tennessee legislature that we weren't going to lay down and let crooked politicians and the left rob us of our history." Plus, Helton crowed, the police escort for his protest had cost the city over $100,000. The legislature's subsequent revoking of the quarter-million-dollar budget line only furthered Helton's sense of the protest's impact.

The protests seemed to provide a pressure-release valve for Helton. During our conversation, he lamented a sense of loss over the last thirty years, a sense that the federal government had conscripted everyone as "slaves" through overregulation and bureaucracy. "I'm in the poor part of the country," he told me. "I'm in the mountains of Arkansas. Wages are fucked here. There're very little jobs in these hole-in-the-wall towns. We chose to be here because we were born and raised here. We know we could go where there's more opportunity but we don't. We could leave but we don't." Helton feels bound to the place through family, through history. A history he feels is now under threat.

Helton lamented all the deaths of the Civil War. "More men died in that war than with the others put together," he said. Didn't that mean something? He felt he could honor the meaning of all that loss by protecting Confederate statues. When I suggested, though, that the statues also represented the enslavement of other people's families, Helton pushed back.

"They don't know what it's like to be a slave any more than I know what it's like to be a slave owner."

It's about the past, it seems, until it isn't.

Toward the end of my conversation with Lee Millar, he had invited me to the monthly meeting of the Sons of Confederate Veterans. I arrived at a Jason's Deli a little east of downtown just before 7 p.m. They hold their monthly meetings in the conference room in the back, where a horseshoe of folding tables lined the outside of the room. The United States flag hung from a flagpole to the left of the lectern, the Confederate flag to the right. Millar had saved me the seat next to him. On my other side sat a large, friendly man named Todd, dressed in a red chamois shirt.

Todd revealed to me, on hearing my accent, that he was from Illinois—a carpetbagger, too. Later he would explain to me how, as a Midwesterner, he came to be involved with the Sons of Confederate Veterans. After marrying a Southern woman and happily making a home in Shelby County, he was invited along to a weekend Civil War reenactment. The prospect of a few days in the woods with the boys seemed like enough fun. The chance to fire a civil-war era cannon sweetened the deal (he did it twice, at $15 a pop). But the clincher was the Sunday service in a clapboard church house: a short sermon, no more than ten minutes, on the parable of the Wise and Foolish Builders. At the conclusion, one of the men came forward to say, "I am Nathan Bedford Forrest and I have built my house on sand." The reenactment of Forrest seeing the light had reflected that light onto Todd. He was hooked. So here he was.

That night's speaker, scheduled to lecture on the Battle of Okolona, hadn't shown. He was on bed rest, announced the camp commander, Alan Doyle—doctor's orders in advance of an urgent coronary artery surgery. The fallback plan was a no-brainer. Since it was the 157th anniversary of the firing on Fort Sumter, we would instead have a roundtable discussion in which we were invited to stand up and share what we knew about those first shots of the war. Many of the participants blamed Lincoln for baiting the South into battle. When a man in a black Henley asked about the fates of other Federal forts in the South, someone referenced Fort Jefferson, on the Florida Gulf Coast which, he reminded us, once held Dr. Mudd—the doctor who had harbored John Wilkes Booth and reset his broken leg, an injury he suffered fleeing Ford's Theatre after murdering the president. There was an outbreak of approving murmurs.

And on it went.

After some housekeeping agenda items, the camp commander ceded the floor to a member who, after apologizing for not being very active recently, sought the camp's recommendation: His pastor, along with 150 other clergy in the city, had signed a letter in support of the removal of Memphis's Confederate monuments. He had sent an email to his pastor, citing scripture that asked who was he to judge, but the pastor's reply, a request to be at peace, was unsatisfactory. He was now in search of a new church. He thanked the camp in advance and took his seat. There was a beat of silence before another member spoke up.

"Me, too."

Then another.

And another.

One man stood up to say that he has come to feel like the only real church exists between him and his King James Bible.

After a few moments of silence, someone finally suggested an Assembly of God congregation in the suburbs and the meeting moved on.

So it had come to this: feeling like they had to choose between their church and Forrest. And many in Camp 215 were choosing Forrest. It's not that they would rather lose their church than lose the statue—they'd already lost the statue. It's the idea, the reverence for the man, they needed. Anything less, it seems, was blasphemy.

TWENTY-SIX

Re-membering

The morning after the SCV meeting, I headed over to the leafy, gothic-revival campus of Rhodes College to talk with Dr. Timothy Huebner. While the Confederates of Memphis abandoned the churches that supported the statue removal, Huebner had just raised a new Forrest marker at his church and, after the previous night, I was even more eager to talk with him about it. Huebner, earnest and warm, wearing rectangular glasses and a tweed jacket, is a history professor at Rhodes and a member of Calvary Episcopal in downtown Memphis, where he'd just organized "A Service of Remembrance and Reconciliation." The service commemorated the unveiling of his new marker about Nathan Bedford Forrest on the sidewalk of a tiny triangular park wedged between the brick-steepled church and its twenty-some parking spaces on Adams Street.

Since 1955, a marker from the Tennessee Historical Commission has stood at the corner of the parking lot, identifying the location as "Forrest's Early Home" in Memphis where "his early business enterprises made him wealthy." And there it stood, uncontested, for sixty years until 2015, when the Lynching Sites Project of Memphis held an interfaith vigil at the marker, drawing attention to a key omission: that those early business enterprises were in the slave trade. Dr. Huebner was at the vigil. It's there that he first noticed the blue placard and its omissions. So began his work to tell a fuller truth about Forrest and what happened there at the corner of Adams Avenue and B.B. King Boulevard.

Soon after the vigil, the church asked Huebner to serve on a neighborhood outreach committee. "And as a professor of history, they asked me to look at the history of the neighborhood." So Huebner, who is white, started digging.

"It didn't take me very long in the archives to figure out that the problem with the sign was not that it didn't simply say what his business was," he explained. Some cursory searches yielded advertisements for Forrest's slave mart, those "early business enterprises" from the 1850s, "and it was that ad that said Adams between Second and Third." Adams between Second and Third? Wait a minute, he thought, that was the same block as Calvary. Could it be that the church, built in 1843, once sat next to Forrest's slave yard?

He kept digging, hunting down property records, then a city map from the 1850s. "I was always entertaining the possibility that I was wrong," he said, wondering if maybe Forrest's slave mart could have been across the street, where the county courthouse stands now, or perhaps the next block over. Not so. He tracked down the plot number: 373, and crossreferenced it on the map. "And that was the moment when I finally knew that this was it." There in the Shelby County archives, bent over the map, Huebner could confirm: his church's parking lot was not just the site of Forrest's home, it was the site of his slave market, too.

"That really hit me for a number of reasons because I saw the extent to which the people who erected that marker in 1955 were covering up something that they knew. Because the very same records that indicate that he had a home there are the ones that indicate that his business was there," he told me. "It's powerful to realize what they knew and what they purposely suppressed. It's also powerful, on a personal level, to think about the fact that the parking lot of the church is the site of where Forrest was buying and selling people."

FORREST BOUGHT THE lot at 87 Adams on the first day of February, 1854. Memphis that year was a universe expanding: The city population had doubled between 1850 and 1854. That year cotton accumulated at the city docks in bales 150 times the number of those shipped out in 1830. And, headed in the opposite direction, enslaved people spent their stopover between the upcountry and the ever-growing Deep South plantations "down the river" in cells at 87 Adams St.

Horatio Eden, who was five years old when he was sold to Forrest, later described the yard as "a kind of square stockade of high boards with two room negro houses around, say, three sides of it and high board fence too high to be scaled on the other side." Cells lined the inside perimeter of the stockade, where those held "were all kept in these rooms, but when an auction was held or buyers came, we were brought out and paraded two by two around a circular brick walk in the center of the stockade. The buyers would stand near by and inspect us as we went by, stop us and examine us: our teeth and limbs."

In early 1858, Forrest bought more space on Adams for his expanding business and his expanding family. He also bought several acres further out in Shelby County and a plantation in

Coahoma, Mississippi. Forrest sent those men, women, and children who were not sold in the lead-up to the planting season to one or the other of these farms to turn a profit from their labor if not from their sale. He was wary of keeping so many bodies in such close quarters in the humid muck of Memphis summer. He was, after all, next door to a church. He then expanded to Vicksburg, overseeing a slave-trading operation with his brothers, bringing in whole gangs from Missouri, making a 20 percent profit on each sale. In the city alderman elections of 1858, hundreds came into the center of the stockade on Adams to nominate their representative from District Three. Forrest won their nomination and, eventually, the election.

In 1860, Forrest ran an ad in *The Memphis Appeal*, stating that "Persons feeling any interest to see genuine native African can be gratified by calling at the negro yard of our friend Forrest, on Adams St." Though the transatlantic slave trade had been abolished for over fifty years by then, the ad claimed "he has for sale, among other negroes, seven direct from Congo." The slave mart, legal and illegal, was "a perfect horror to all negroes far and near," the *New-York Tribune* wrote, where Forrest and his brother beat men "until blood trickled to the ground" and women were whipped with a heavy leather thong dipped in a bucket of salt water. Over one thousand enslaved people passed through his "slave mart" each year, whose sale netted Forrest $50,000 (that's one million dollars a year, adjusted for inflation) each year he was in business.

But, for the past sixty-three years, when anyone pulled into the parking lot for the 10 a.m. service at Calvary or waited at the nearby bus stop for the eastbound local, all they'd be invited to consider were "Forrest's early business enterprises."

Huebner wanted to change that.

So he began to share his findings with the church and with friends. One friend, Phyllis Aluko, a public defender in Shelby County and a board member of the Memphis chapter of the NAACP, told him about her work to erect a marker at the site of the 1866 Memphis Massacre—a three-day eruption of racial violence that began as a fight between Black Union soldiers and Irish-American police officers that left 46 Black people dead, nearly 300 injured, and over 100 Black schools, houses, and churches burned. Why not erect your own marker and counter the old, obfuscating one already there? Aluko suggested. Tell the truth about the space.

With a group of students in his history seminar, Huebner began to work on the text for a new marker. "As we got further into it, it became apparent to me that we needed to do a service at the church and it needed to be a service of remembrance and reconciliation," he said. "I wanted us to try to remember this history and specifically to remember the lives of the people who were sold there." The English word *remember* comes to us from late Latin and old French, "to bring to mind again," but Huebner offered another way of thinking about the term: "To *re*-member in the sense that you're putting that back together. That's the process of doing the research: you are trying to *re*-member this story and to *re*-member the lives of these people. So we wanted to do the research on their names and know who they were so we could use these names in the service in order to make the point that these were human beings who had lives and they had names and they had ages."

The ceremony, "A Service of Remembrance and Reconciliation," took place on April 4, 2018, fifty years to the day since the assassination of Martin Luther King, Jr. just a mile south of Calvary, on the balcony of the Lorraine Motel. Six hundred people filled the pews, crowded in behind the last row, and spilled out into the lobby.

"I'm glad that this fuller truth will be told for many decades to passersby," the Reverend Scott Walters, the rector at Calvary, told the crowd. "The uncomfortable tension this story exposes may be more poignantly ours as the people of Calvary church than anyone else's," he continued. "And it can change us if we let it." The racial caste system of the antebellum South, he noted, was a part of the ordinariness of life to most white Memphians of the time, as it was for those parishioners of the church, in those days—just the water in which they swam. "Illusions are invisible to most of us who hold them. That's what makes them illusions." But he cautioned that "our temptation today may be to make monsters out of our Christian forebears and imagine that maybe we could never be so blind to such horrors. This is a dangerous illusion as well."

Rev. Walters then told the crowd that a series of people would come to the pulpit to read the names of seventy-eight men, women, and children—the names of some who had been bought and sold at Forrest's slave mart. It was a way, he explained, to honor them, to provide, in a small and simple way, a dignity once denied them. But it was also a way to offer a confession, a way for those gathered to "drop an illusion of innocence and to restore a proper tension to our lives as we wonder together what in Memphis and what in America and what in this world should be unsettling my prayers today."

Dr. Charles McKinney, chair of Africana Studies at Rhodes College, rose to the pulpit. "Names of the enslaved sold at

Eighty-seven Adams, 1854 to 1862," he said as the church bell began a steady toll, marking time and tribute. Into its ring, McKinney began to read: "Jerry, age thirty-five. Charles, age forty-five. Dick, age fourteen. Paige, age nine. Washington, age twenty. Catherine, age twenty-three. John Henry, age three. Mary Ann, age three."

From the second lectern across the sanctuary, Beverly Bond continued reading. As she recited the next name—"Tom, age sixteen"—a small but remarkable thing happened: someone stood up. A balding man in chinos and sport coat rose, his hands clasped in front of him, his head down. The whole gravity of the room, already trembling, shifted in that moment. Our history, and all its weight, was embodied, re-membered, in the sanctuary. By the time Bond read the name "Solomon, age twenty," people throughout the church were standing. And when Tami Sawyer's voice briefly broke between the "twenty" and "one" of a man named Ishmael's age, everyone in the church was on their feet.

People choked back sobs, the bell tolled, and Sawyer read on: "Harrison, age sixteen. Wilson, age eight. John, age twenty-five."

The service was an American elegy set to the toll of the church bell. It created a space for honesty about America's past and our present, where those in the church could see and feel what whiteness has wrought in a more urgent, human way. It was not a "Kumbaya" moment but something both smaller and more honest—a simple gesture, profoundly urgent and profoundly basic, redolent of dignity and grief and shame and love and horror and confession and good and evil and the Devil and God—in other words, it was wholly American. And thus befitting a ceremony meant to restore the tension of the country's original sin. It was a start. It suggested a way to re-understand American history, grounded in the acknowledgment of the names and ages and lives lived and robbed in this space. This campaign to tell the truth about Forrest also revealed the truth about ourselves. Who we've been, who we are, who we might yet be. And maybe, at this late hour, even as so many Neo-Confederates were retreating from that knowledge, maybe more of us were arriving there to accept it.

THE NEW MARKER in Calvary's parking lot, like the old marker in Calvary's parking lot, stands just across the street from the county courthouse. The new wrought-iron marker describes the scale and importance of the slave trade to the city of Memphis in the years leading up to the outbreak of the Civil War, highlighting the importance of Forrest's slave mart in that human trafficking. Van Turner, the county commissioner who now owns the park where the Forrest statue once stood and where his body is still buried, has practiced law in that courthouse for years. He would bristle whenever he saw that previous sign and its word choice, he told me. It was as if they were saying, "We're going to parade this right before your faces and dare [you] not to do anything about it."

So, the new sign is, for him, a welcome change. And it made me wonder: Was it surreal, now, owning the gravesite of the man who became a rich man trafficking humans across the street from where he practices law? It's a question he's been asking himself lately, too.

"The great grandchild of slaves now owns the park where Forrest, who fought to maintain slavery, is buried. Who fought to keep slavery alive. A hundred and fifty years later the very thing you wanted has been flipped upside down," he reflected. It made him think about a quote from Dr. King, from the speech he delivered on the steps of the Alabama state capitol at the successful completion of the Selma to Montgomery march in 1965: "The arc of the moral universe is long but it bends toward justice."

So, no, Turner told me, it's not surreal. "It's the arc."

LIKE A LOT of people over the past couple of years, I've careened wildly between hope and despair. Every so often, deep down a rabbit hole in an archive, or in the middle of an interview, or lost in thought on a long drive, I would catch myself compulsively updating a mental ledger of optimism and pessimism, as if I were plotting coordinates on the moral universe as I puttered around the Southeast. Forrest back in Selma: despair. Forrest Hall still Forrest Hall: despair. But an awakened political consciousness on the MTSU campus among students both Black and white: hope. Jack Kershaw cutting a swath of unreconstructed racism through the twentieth century: despair. Tami Sawyer, fist raised on the empty pedestal: hope. Unite the Right, Trump, Huebner . . . you get the idea.

So when Van Turner—who now owns the park where it was once illegal for his father to walk—says it's the arc, I was inclined to agree. An informed optimism about the state of the country, the universe. It felt right. Like a good ending.

At least for a while.

It was something from the Service of Remembrance and Reconciliation that lingered with me and that would eventually push me to reconsider ending with Turner's words. I spoke with

Rev. Dorothy Wells, the rector at another Episcopal church in Memphis, who had written the prayers recited that day after the reading of the names. I remarked on how much her prayers emphasized the importance of awareness, especially for white people. As if to say: it was one thing to nod in somber recognition of injustices past, it's another to trace those injustices into the present and ask how they have shaped you. And to do so without the benefit of hindsight, without the moral clarity of 150 years' distance.

"I do think that there is a need for folks who are not of African descent but who have in any way, shape, or form benefitted not only from slavery but from systemic racism that has survived beyond slavery, to be able to acknowledge that," she explained. But not by taking blame for the actions of an ancestor; it's not about blame—placing it or taking it. Instead, Wells said, the idea is to see past an individual's feelings or actions to the systems built to protect the privilege and fortune amassed by some through the deprivation of others. We have to recognize the injury and care about those who have been harmed, she said, then we have to see the systems that produce and perpetuate those injuries. And to do that, we need to use our sense of the past to hone our awareness of the present.

So, not to undercut commissioner Turner; for him it is the arc, no doubt. But as I reflected on what Wells was saying, as I felt the tension between my life and Forrest's continue to grow tighter, I was reminded that, for so long, people like Forrest (which is to say people like me) have been the force heaving against that arc's bend. Our very identity was invented to be a bulwark against that bend. Better, then, to understand what happened in Memphis not as a triumph, an end, but rather as a beginning. To try to divine a cosmic optimism or pessimism out of the campaign is to miss the point.

In my conversation with Wells, she pointed to Memphis—a city that is 63 percent African American, where nearly 30 percent of African Americans live below the poverty line. Many of the state's failing schools are located in the city's African American communities. That's not by accident. "But it's easy not to see that," said Wells, "because a lot of that poverty is concentrated into certain neighborhoods, so people don't see it. It's not something that ever comes near you." Seeing the wrong in the thirty-foot bronze statue of an infamous man standing in a city park or the slave market in the parking lot—those are layups. The #TakeEmDown901 campaign and "A Service for Remembrance and Reconciliation" showed that plenty of white people were ready to forego the palliative provided by the Forrest statue. But what about the work to tear down the "thought monuments," the structural forces that create the benefit of the doubt in interactions with police officers and prosecutors and judges? Or campaigns to address segregated schools with uneven funding? Lobbying to combat voter suppression? The opportunity gap? The wealth gap?

A symbol is gone; the systems remain.

And we've made hard work of the easy part. In the scheme of things, the monument campaigns have cost very little. The upcoming battles will cost much more. If we want to get to the "beyond," if we want to unknot whiteness from its implied supremacy, if we want to rebuild the country on lines other than those drawn to impose and protect that supremacy, if we want to close a 10-1 racial wealth gap, or create equal access to quality schools and healthcare and the ballot box, if we want to fight for a $15 minimum wage or end mass incarceration, these campaigns will require sacrifices—not the least of them material sacrifices— far beyond what the Confederate monument debate has cost us.

Even so, to summon the will among enough Americans to address these issues, we must first come to a common understanding of the past—an understanding grounded in the acknowledgement of all that has been taken in the name of whiteness. And, in that way, the campaign and the service are a good beginning.

ON MY LAST reporting trip to Memphis, I paid one more visit to Health Sciences Park and to the empty pedestal. It was high spring, the cars parked along Manassas Street dusted with pollen. The park is just down the street from Sun Studios, the famous record label run by Sam Phillips that recorded the likes of Howlin' Wolf, Johnny Cash, and the King himself, Elvis Presley. Before his audition with Sun in 1954, the story goes that Presley anxiously paced the blocks around the studio. I've often wondered if he walked past the Forrest statue, compulsively patting down his ducktail haircut before heading into the studio to sing "Without You." In his essay on Elvis, "Elvis: Presliad," Greil Marcus writes about the difficulty of pinpointing watershed moments in a person's life. "You can't answer such questions, not computer-style," Marcus writes. "But you have no claim on the story unless you risk a guess."

So here's my guess about Forrest's life.

It takes place back before he even came to Memphis, while he was still living in Mississippi, working for his Uncle

Jonathan—until the duel with the three Matlocks in the town square that would claim his uncle's life. Forrest, remember, inherited Jonathan's debt, which was, as Jonathan had put it, "greater as I apprehend than I will be able to pay." Everything flows from that moment on the corner in Hernando: Forrest, in the red, soon opts to go full-time into the slave trade, where he makes a fortune. It's with that fortune that he's able to equip his own regiment when the war comes. It's as a cavalry leader that he distinguishes himself as a cunning, instinctive military mind. It's as a distinguished Confederate general that he's tapped to head the Klan. It's as the head of the Klan that he endeavors to "redeem" the South, making it possible for them to reinstitute white supremacist rule, and to set about hoisting statues to their heroes.

You can drop the needle on all of it right there on the square in Hernando. Of course, it all rests on the unshakable belief that the men and women Forrest bought and sold into enslavement were subhuman. But many in America have held and hold such beliefs. We know about Forrest, specifically, because he was born poor on the frontier and availed himself of the opportunities to advance in a country and an economy built on the backs of others. (You might say he pulled himself up by his bootstraps, but those bootstraps were other human beings.) He steps into that role, into history, and onto many a pedestal when he unholsters his six-shooter that afternoon in Hernando.

Part of me wishes there were a statue of Forrest that captured that moment. Desperate, violent, bleeding from the arm. The weight of the mortgages suspended above him, a spent revolver in one hand, a bowie knife in the other, surrounded by death and debt, just before he makes the crossroads wager for material wealth at that devilish price. How American. This is a truer American story than most white people tell. And it's probably why we don't tell this one very often. There was no rich sailor to teach him the ways of the upper crust, no million-dollar loan from a father. Just the striving young white man, desperate for wealth, taking on the weight and the horror of the slave trade and signing on to the bargain white America plays with capitalism.

The story is a reminder that the deep inequities in our system, like the ones Rev. Wells had pointed to, didn't come about by accident. They're the result of a sustained campaign to use race as a way to extract and hoard resources. That audition Presley was going to when he paced around this block in Memphis? It was to fill a role Sam Phillips had long imagined, and would often fantasize about to his assistant: "If I could find a white man who had the Negro sound and the Negro feel, I could make a billion dollars!"

Like I said, this book begins and ends with an empty pedestal. What started in Selma with a bare granite column where a bust of Forrest was about to be replaced ends three years later with the vacant marble base on the south side of a Memphis park. But in the ending, too, there is another beginning. The empty pedestal should serve as a reminder of all that's been taken, of all the debts still owed. Revising the city's landscape to tell the truth about Forrest, to restore the tension between his life and ours, is a start. But it is only a start.

The Two-Face God
Montgomery

It's a muggy day in late April, 2018, and I'm standing in the central courtyard of the National Memorial for Peace and Justice, overlooking downtown Montgomery, Alabama. From this vantage point (on some of the highest ground in the city), I can see the state capitol building and the bank towers below, the pine banks of the Alabama River a little further on. But I'm standing here to take in the more immediate setting: the 805 steel markers that surround me. The memorial hallows this high ground for the approximately 4400 victims of racial terror lynchings that took place in America between 1877 and 1950. There's one marker for each county in which a lynching took place, each inscribed with the names and dates of those men, women, and children murdered for being Black in America. Some markers include a single name, while others, like Shelby County, Tennessee—Memphis's county—list twenty. Selma's county, Dallas, lists nineteen names.

I'm here for the memorial's opening weekend, just four days after Confederate Memorial Day (still a state holiday in Alabama; I didn't have to work). Montgomery is like this: competing histories, held in discomfiting proximity. Monday off in honor of

Confederates, Friday afternoon at a lynching memorial. Dr. King's old church, just around the corner from the First White House of the Confederacy. It's paradoxes like these that led Jason McCall, a poet from Montgomery, to refer to the city as the "two-face God." And up here, at the center of this memorial, high on the hillside, you're closest to the two-face god of Montgomery's—and America's—history.

It's been just three weeks since Calvary Episcopal dedicated their new Forrest marker in Memphis. Like Calvary, the Memorial for Peace and Justice tells a fuller truth about our past, with plans to revise not just Montgomery's landscape, but also the country's.

The memorial is a project of the Equal Justice Initiative (EJI), a Montgomery-based nonprofit founded by attorney Bryan Stevenson. Originally established to guarantee legal representation to the state's death-row inmates, the EJI has expanded its work in recent years, seeking to address the root causes of the racial bias the lawyers encounter daily in the criminal justice system, from excessive sentencing to overpolicing and abuse. In 2015, as a part of their expanding work, the EJI published "Lynching in America: Confronting the Legacy of Racial Terror." Their research identified 800 more lynchings than previous totals. Many took place in the American South, but not all. There were lynchings in Minnesota, Illinois, Maryland. And the EJI argues that this era of violence functioned as a link in an unbroken chain of systemic racism, from slavery to mass incarceration. And furthermore, that for all the monuments, plaques, and statues that lionize the Confederacy, there remained a conspicuous collective silence around these lynchings. The EJI sought to change this, positing that "There is a path to recovery and reconciliation when we tell the truth about our history in the public square."

With the Memorial for Peace and Justice, the EJI has created that public square. It is both a major contribution to memorial architecture and a provocative intervention into American memory. From the entrance gate, down the sloping lawn from the central pavilion, the rows of markers appear as columns. It gives the memorial a neoclassical look, reminiscent of a colonnade, or a steel interpretation of the Parthenon. And a walk through the first hallway seems to confirm that sense. The markers are made of corten steel, weathered to a burnt ocher. Six feet tall, they stand flush with the floor, connected to the ceiling by a pole. They are arranged in offset rows, so there's no clear path through—no matter how you proceed, you wind up face to face with a marker, with the history and the violence it commemorates.

It wasn't until I turned the first corner of the memorial that I realized that the markers did not, in fact, bear the weight of the roof. The floor of the second hallway sloped downward, but the markers kept their level. As I descended, it seemed as though the markers were rising above me. As I moved, the memorial moved. And it was only then that I saw them for what they are: not columns but gallows.

It's worth noting: the term "racial terror lynching" is used here to distinguish from other public hangings of the era, like those that took place in the Old West, perpetrated by vigilantes in communities where criminal justice systems had yet to be implemented. The lynchings commemorated here specifically targeted people of color and occurred in places where there was an established criminal justice system. And they took place without intervention from—and often were condoned by—that system. Indeed, men and women of color were regularly murdered on the courthouse lawn for crimes such as wearing a military uniform or bumping into a white person on the street, and less than 1 percent of those responsible for the violence were ever held to account. For over a century, the federal government failed to pass antilynching legislation; finally, a largely symbolic bill was passed the year after the memorial's opening. All told, these public-spectacle murders served as a reminder to whole communities of how American society was structured. And how that structure was enforced. They were, in short, terrorism.

By the time I'd reached the end of the second corridor, the markers hung far above my head, stock-still and looming. I stood beneath them, looking up. This vantage point is no accident. A sign on one wall informs that a 1920 lynching in Duluth, Minnesota, drew a crowd of thousands. Another, in Waco, Texas, a few years earlier, brought out 15,000. Often at museums, my impulse is to project myself into the story, to make it personal. At the Holocaust museum in Washington, you are even given an ID card of someone whose story you follow through the exhibitions. Standing at the bottom of the second corridor of this memorial, the relation becomes clear—my surrogates are the men and women who committed, attended, bought postcards of these lynchings. By positioning me so, the design of the memorial insists that I acknowledge this connection. White Americans' potential to change, to create a more equitable and peaceful future, the EJI argues, depends on our ability to claim this history as our own, to understand ourselves in its context. Here, underground, under these markers, the memorial asks us to take the weight, confront the racial violence that anchors American life, or we will never get out from under it.

At the end of the pavilion's circuit, I passed through an opening that led me to the courtyard, where I scaled the mound and could look out over the memorial and see how it framed the view of everything beyond it. In 77 years, 4400 lynchings. That averages to a lynching every six days—roughly one every week. For 77 years. Every week from the end of Reconstruction to the dawn of the civil rights movement, every week from the circus debut of the human cannonball to the announcement of possible rocket flights to the moon, every week from Forrest's death to my mother's birth, white Americans lynched Black Americans so that we could be white. So much changed in that time; our psychosis about race did not. Standing in the center of the memorial, the markers all around me, the point was clear: racial terror was the clockwork of America life.

Even having read the EJI's report and having spent the past several years tracing Forrest's life and legacy through American life—one that's bound up in so many moments of racial reckoning—still, surveying the rows of markers, I was astounded, bereft. As I climbed down the central mound in the courtyard, I realized why I kept swallowing and sucking my teeth as I moved through the memorial: all that weathered steel tasted like blood in my mouth.

OUTSIDE THE PAVILION, I found duplicates of each of the markers, laid out horizontally like coffins awaiting burial— the "memory bank," as the memorial's design team calls it. Every

248   *Down Along with That Devil's Bones*

county is invited to claim the marker and display it at the site of a lynching. Just as the memorial moves as we move, the memory bank will change as we change. And the unclaimed markers will remain here, in rebuke of those counties who have looked away once more from this past. Ignoring this history leaves a mark, too. The memorial will become not just a repository for a broader collective memory, but for our collective forgetting, too.

There is, of course, the inevitable counterargument: 1877 to 1950? That's over and done. But by gut-checking some 800 American counties, the memorial challenges any easy assumption about the inevitability of progress. And it prompts questions about what became of those who committed these lynchings, attended them, or turned a blind eye to them? And what happened to their children? What happened to the systems of power that condoned them, required them? What happened to the story told to justify these actions and inactions? Was there some grand transformation? When?

Laid out horizontally, these duplicate markers call to mind the grid of boxes that make up Berlin's Holocaust Memorial, another city using its physical space to grapple with its past. Likewise, the vertically arranged markers in the memorial reference the pillars that front the Apartheid Museum in South Africa—part of that country's larger project of truth and reconciliation. No such commission has ever been convened in the United States to reckon the toll of our own apartheid. The Memorial to Peace and Justice puts forward one ledger to be accounted for.

In this way, the memorial is an architectural embodiment of Bryan Stevenson's argument that truth and reconciliation are sequential. Thus, no overtures are made to reconciliation here.

You are not meant to be consoled, but rather to be confronted. The white American instinct to move toward absolution and innocence is short-circuited here. Instead, in the memorial's very design, visitors are forced to grapple with their place in a system of disenfranchisement, violence, and moral oblivion. Otherwise, so many of us would have only the flimsiest sense of what needed to be reckoned. If we have no idea of who we've been, we have no idea who we are. And thus have no hope of changing. The memorial is a dynamic testament to the idea that a country cannot escape its history. Rather, it must be faced, so that, as the memorial's designer Michael Murphy argues, "Our nation will begin to heal from over a century of silence."

AFTER I FINISHED walking through the memorial, I was shaken, not yet ready to head home. So I took a walk around the surrounding neighborhood. Next door to the entrance of the memorial is an Alabama State parole office. The two-face God at work again. From there, I climbed down the hill to the banks of the Alabama River. Where the river bends to a U, a sign informed that in 1961, after days of torrential rain, the river flooded to a point marked there where I stood. I looked left and right, unable to find the high-water line. But then I looked up. High on a pole above me, like the mast of a ship, was the mark. So high—58 feet, 1 inch, to be precise—that I had to crane my neck the whole way back to see it.

Biblical, the amount of water that fell in 1961—just five years after Officer Day, my predecessor, arrested Rosa Parks down the street from where I stood, and a century after Forrest left the plantation for the cavalry. It occurred to me that, for years, as I chased Forrest's memory across the country, it was Forrest, more than anyone else, who has taught me the meaning of *whiteness* in America. The battles over his monuments, on the other hand, point a way forward, show how we might learn to be another way.

In Roman mythology, it is Janus, the two-face God, who presides over transitions—the beginnings and the endings of wars, of births and deaths. And, really, the tension between the monument and the memorial is one of life and death. The monument immortalizes; the memorial mourns. Confederate monuments believe that God will vindicate us, that we are already redeemed by history, that there is nothing for which to account. They strike a defensive posture that refuses to dig into the darker aspects of the past, wants both faces to look away. Memorials like the one in Montgomery ask Americans to forego such beliefs, and instead ask us to grieve, to sit in the weight of who we have been, and to let that weight mold our sense of who we are. Memorials, in other words, want to hold us to account. Fitting then, that the Memorial for Peace and Justice is located in Montgomery, both the cradle of the Confederacy and the birthplace of the civil rights movement. Out of the tumult of the city of the two-face God, the Equal Justice Initiative is charting a course toward a possible peace.

A BREEZE COMING in off the bend in the river brought to mind the raft ride that took Forrest from President's Island back to mainland Memphis to die. "The same night they buried him, there came a storm," wrote journalist Lafcadio Hearn, who had stopped in Memphis on his way to New Orleans that day. From his hotel room, Hearn watched the storm come in and "somehow or other the queer fancy came to me that the dead Confederate cavalrymen, rejoined by their desperate leader, were fighting ghostly battles with the men who died for the Union."

That ghostly battle still rages. Same war, same general. Storms gather, waters rise. Ending this war will require a moral clarity about the meaning and consequence of America's past—one that few Americans have proved capable of. Because simply knowing our history cannot redeem us, cannot, as they say in Selma, get us to the "beyond." Knowledge alone cannot make the nation more just or equitable, nor does it create or change policy. Knowledge alone cannot undo what's been done in white America's name. What a clear-eyed sense of American history can do, however, is show us how to look forward and backward at the same time, to see how the past marks the present like the waterline left after a flood. If we hear, in the sally port's clang, the echoes of President's Island; feel, in the pull of the voting booth's curtain, the brush of the calico mask; see, in the diverging lines of American wealth, the logbooks of the Adams Street Negro Mart; then, even at this eleventh hour, we might remember the country more fully, and in so doing, join in the work of reconstructing it.

ACKNOWLEDGMENTS

First, I'd like to thank everyone who spoke to me for this book. I am grateful to all of you for sharing your stories and your insight, without which this book would not exist.

To Chip Brantley and Andrew Beck Grace: thank you for all the advice, friendship, and calls at the shop. I hope you find some cinnamon here.

Thanks also to my many teachers. Through his encouragement and support, his patience and guidance, L. Lamar Wilson gave this project life. Thanks to Michael Martone, for the gift of anecdotage; here it is, come back to you. To Kiese Laymon, for showing me the power and responsibility of revision. I am forever indebted. Eve Dunbar once asked me to consider what it means to be alive to American history. A decade later, I hazard this book as an answer.

A heartfelt "Roll Tide" to everyone at the University of Alabama—especially Joel Brouwer, Wendy Rawlings, James Andrew Crank, Kellie Wells, Hali Felt, and Utz McKnight.

I am especially grateful to my editors, Betsy Gleick and Chuck Adams, whose insights, care, and direction have shaped and improved this book considerably. And to Melissa Flashman, at Janklow & Nesbit, for seeing the potential in this book and then advocating for it every step of the way.

I have been buoyed by the friendship and counsel of Andrew Stevens, Nabila Lovelace, Nate Hardy, Brian Oliu, Briana Markoff, Kyes Stevens, Joe Lucido, Kit Emslie, P. J. Williams, Ryan Bollenbach, Brian Slagle, Graham Smith, Stephen O'Neill, Zachary Towne-Smith, and Nathan Towne-Smith—a million thanks to them for chewing the cud, kicking the tires, and keeping the faith.

To my parents, Daniel O'Neill and Sally Towne: thank you for instilling in me a sense of curiosity, for fostering a sense of engagement with the world, and for handing down that dusty old sedan. I hope this book makes you proud.

And, finally, to Shaelyn Smith, for the butter and the bread: thank you, thank you.

NOTES

I relied on Jack Hurst's *Nathan Bedford Forrest: A Biography* for much of the basic information about Forrest. Hurst provides a comprehensive, objective chronicle of the general's complicated life. Paul Ashdown and Edward Caudill's *The Myth of Nathan Bedford Forrest* assembles a clear picture of Forrest's afterlife—his legacy and legend—and it proved equally useful in the writing of this book. Biographical information was rounded out by Brian Steele Wills's *A Battle From the Start: The Life of Nathan Bedford Forrest*, and Andrew Nelson Lytle's *Bedford Forrest and His Critter Company*—the former for its information on Forrest's role in the Klan, the latter for the way Lytle channels the emotional resonance of Forrest's life. Just as Stephen Colbert used to "feel the news at you," Lytle does the same with Forrest.

Erika Doss's *Memorial Mania: Public Feeling in America* was essential in understanding the history and cultural function of monuments and memorials. Likewise, I relied on Colin Rafferty's *Hallow This Ground* for its delineation of monuments and memorials, and as a model for negotiating the personal and the political while writing about them. Dell Upton's *What Can and Can't Be Said: Race, Uplift, and Monument Building in the Contemporary South* provided a framework for charting the tensions between

Civil War and civil rights memorials, with special attention to Selma's symbolic landscape. Dr. Derek H. Alderman, both in his scholarship and in conversation with me, deepened my sense of how memorializing the past inevitably reveals power struggles in the present.

A number of writers and thinkers helped to shape my understanding of race—its social construction and its very real consequences. Among them were James Baldwin (especially his essay "The White Man's Guilt"), Nikole Hannah-Jones and her reporting on school segregation, Lillian Smith's *Killers of the Dream*, Noel Ignatiev and John Garner's work in the journal *Race Traitor*, John Biewen and Chenjerai Kumanyika's podcast series *Seeing White*, Robin DiAngelo's *White Fragility: Why It's So Hard for White People to Talk about Racism*, Nell Irvin Painter's *The History of White People*, and Patty McIntosh's essay "White Privilege: Unpacking the Invisible Knapsack."

Throughout the book, I attempted to be as transparent as possible in my sourcing of information. Occasionally, though—for the sake of a sentence's rhythm or, because of the sheer number of names and dates and titles to keep track of in this book, out of mercy for the reader—I opted not to cite a source in text. I've included those works here.

PART ONE

Edward E. Baptist's *The Half Has Never Been Told: Slavery and the Making of American Capitalism* deeply informed my understanding of the economic and political situation in the years leading up to the Civil War—emphasizing just how catalytic and cataclysmic the slave system was. Jill Lepore's *These Truths: A History of the United States* set the tensions of the Civil War in a longer context, striking at the central paradox of American notions of freedom and pointing up the enduring questions of the nation: By what sources do Americans draw power? Who is the "we" in "we the people"? References made to the wealth generated on West Indian plantations and the history of the slave trade in New England are also sourced from her book. I've been guided throughout by her credo that "The past is an inheritance, a gift and a burden. It can't be shirked. You carry it everywhere. There's nothing for it but to get to know it."

John Hardy's antebellum history *Selma: Her Institutions and Her Men* helped me to localize these broader American themes in Alabama's Black Belt region. Information on Elodie and Nathaniel Dawson came from *Practical Strangers: The Courtship Correspondence of Nathaniel Dawson and Elodie Todd, Sister of Mary Todd Lincoln,* a collection edited by Stephen Berry and Angela Esco Elder. Biographical information on Benjamin Turner is sourced from Alston Fitts's book *Selma: A Bicentennial History.* Fitts's patience and generosity over the course of several interviews is also deeply appreciated. Brigadier General Edward Winslow's letter, referenced in Chapter Two, I found included in *The War of the Rebellion: A Compilation of the Official Records of the Union and Confederate Armies.*

I relied on David Blight's work—in book and lecture form—to better understand the Civil War's legacy and the consequences of its disputed memories.

I'd also like to extend my gratitude to the Selma Dallas County Public Library—their collections of city council minutes, microfilm, and newspaper clipping files provided the foundation of my research into the 2000 mayoral election and the Forrest statue's dedication, theft, and replacement. Alvin Benn, journeyman reporter, chronicled this saga in a series of particularly enlightening articles for *The Montgomery Advertiser* included in the library's collection. Thanks also to librarian Stephen Posey for his help.

PART TWO

My understanding of the stakes of recent college campus protests was shaped, in no small part, by three scholarly essays. Historical context for the reemergence of Confederate symbols came from Logan Strother, Spencer Piston, and Thomas Ogorzalek's essay "Pride or Prejudice?: Racial Prejudice, Southern Heritage, and White Support for the Confederate Battle Flag" published in the *Du Bois Review.* Stephen Clowney's essay "Landscape Fairness: Removing Discimination from the Built Environment" mapped that history onto monuments and memorials. Jordan P. Brasher, Derek H. Alderman, and Joshua F.J. Inwood's essay "Applying Critical Race and Memory Studies to University Place Naming Controversies: Toward a Responsible Landscape Policy" offered a deeper context for the debates on American college campuses with a useful theory of a "hidden curriculum" reflected in the names and statuary of a campus.

As noted in the text, Court Carney's work on the history and historiography of Nathan Bedford Forrest was indispensable. In "The Most Man in the World: Nathan Bedford Forrest and the Cult of Masculinity in the South" and other essays and publications, Carney astutely lays out the complexity of Forrest's legacy, its contingencies, and its evolution.

The Confederate and Neo-Confederate Reader, edited by James W. Lowen and Edward H. Sebesta, collects primary sources from both the Confederacy and its latter-day acolytes. The speeches, documents, and essays collected there make clear the animating force of the war for the Confederacy: the preservation and expansion of slavery.

The Albert Gore Center and the Middle Tennessee State University Heritage Center provided me with documents on the history of the school, its entanglement with Forrest, and its freighted connection to the surrounding community. The Forrest Hall Protest Collection, in the Digital Collections at Walker Library, MTSU, is a rich resource of information. In particular, "A Confederate on Campus: Nathan Bedford Forrest as MTSU's Mascot," by Josh Howard, and the essays of Elizabeth Catte deepened the historical context of the 2015–2016 campaign to change the name of Forrest Hall from students' points of view. All told, the Gore Center's collection was a researcher's dream.

Thanks also to *Daily News Journal*, whose coverage of the 2015–2016 campaign helped me to keep a finger on the pulse of the Middle Tennessee community.

PART THREE

Neil R. McMillen's *The Citizens' Council: Organized Resistance to the Second Reconstruction, 1954–64* set Jack Kershaw's work in broader context of the "massive resistance" to the legislative gains of the civil rights movement.

For information on more recent resistance to civil rights, I relied on the Southern Poverty Law Center and their blog *Hatewatch*. Ryan Lenz's reporting on the League of the South's evolution proved especially crucial.

Robyn Semien and Zoe Chace's reporting on the aftermath of the Charlottesville rally for the PRX radio show *This American Life* oriented me to the machinations of the event's planners in the lead-up to the rally.

Likewise, online media collective *Unicorn Riot*'s invaluable work in assembling and publishing documents about the planning of the Unite the Right rally furthered my understanding of the goals of the rally, while their collection of footage from that day allowed me to see the chaos unfold from multiple points of view.

Bradley Dean Griffin's commentaries on his blog, *Occidental Dissent*, and his various social media accounts provided useful information about the League of the South's evolving role in the Confederate monument debate and proved to be as illuminating as it was disturbing. Michael Hill also maintains a prolific online presence that helped me to better understand how he sought to position and recruit for the League of the South.

As Chapter Two makes clear, Elaine Frantz Parsons' book *Ku Klux: The Birth of the Klan During Reconstruction* deeply informed my understanding of the procedures and public posturings of the early Klan.

The anecdote from Chapter Two about the "bottom rail on top" exchange comes from James McPherson's *Battle Cry of Freedom: The Civil War Era*—a terrific single-volume history of the war. The quote from Simon Elder there comes from Volume

Seven of the "Report of the Joint Select Committee to Inquire into the Condition of Affairs in the Late Insurrectionary States." The anecdote about the Birmingham Klan screening *Birth of a Nation* comes from Gary May's book *The Informant: The FBI, The Ku Klux Klan, and the Murder of Viola Liuzzo.* The reference to the murders during the constitutional conventions comes from Adam Gopnik's essay in *The New Yorker* (April 8, 2019) on Reconstruction, "How the South Won the Civil War." The passage regarding the League of the South's pressure on Albemarle officials to charge Harris and Long is sourced from Tess Owens's reporting at *Vice News.*

PART FOUR

The archives of the Benjamin L. Hooks Public Library in Memphis were a valuable resource while writing this book. Their clipping files contain a century and a half of newspaper articles about Forrest and his legend. Their digital collection includes the pamphlet published by the Forrest Monument Association titled *The Forrest Monument: Its History and Dedication; A Memorial in Art, Oratory and Literature.* It is from here that I source the information on the statue's production process and dedication in Chapter Three. Their microfilm collection includes the *Appeal* article describing the reinterment of Forrest and his wife, also in that chapter.

I drew on much of Ida B. Wells-Barnett's work, including *The Red Record: Tabulated Statistics and Alleged Causes of Lynching in the United States* and *Southern Horrors: Lynch Law in All Its Phases.* I relied on Paula Giddins's *Ida: A Sword Among Lions* for supplemental biographical information. John Cimprich's *Fort Pillow, a Civil War Massacre, and Public Memory* and Andrew Ward's *River Run Red: The Fort Pillow Massacre in the American Civil War* provided a foundation for understanding the Fort Pillow massacre and its contested place in public memory. Wendi C. Thomas's MLK50.com project produced insightful, thoughtful coverage of the #TakeEmDown901 campaign and connected it to broader social-justice movements in the city. Likewise, the reporting of the Memphis *Commercial Appeal* was crucial in following the yearslong, labyrinthine process of removing the statue from Health Sciences Park. (A brief exhortation to the reader, if I may: Subscribe to your local newspaper!) Nate DiMeo's *Memory Palace* podcast's episode on the Forrest statue in Memphis is, in DiMeo's typical style, informative, lyrical, and gutting. Listening to that episode in the summer of 2015 made me think that my idea about Forrest statues could hold a book.